Shadows & Ink

VOL. 2

JOE MYNHARDT

Published by Crystal Lake Publishing
Tales from The Darkest Depths

Website: www.crystallakepub.com

WELCOME
TO ANOTHER

CRYSTAL LAKE PUBLISHING
CREATION

Contents

Section 1

Advanced Writing Techniques

Chapter 1

Psychological Horror vs. Gore

Let's delve into a topic that fascinates and, let's admit it, sometimes confuses even the best of us: the subtle dance between psychological horror and gore. At the heart of every horror story lies a choice between the unseen terrors that lurk in the shadows of our minds and the visceral, blood-soaked scenes that make our stomachs churn.

Understanding Psychological Horror

Imagine this scenario: You're nestled comfortably in your home, the world outside quiet and at peace. A creak echoes through the halls, jarring in the silence. Your heart skips a beat. You check, and yet, there's nothing but the stillness of the night greeting you. That shiver running down your spine? That's the essence of psychological horror. It's a genre that doesn't rely on visible monsters or gory scenes but rather on the unseen, the untold, and the unexplained. It's the art of crafting tension and fear from what might be lurking just out of sight, rather than what's right in front of your eyes.

Psychological horror is a masterful game of cat and mouse played with the reader's mind. It's an intricate dance of shadows, where what's not shown is just as important as what is. This genre thrives on the uncertainty and fear of the unknown. It's not about the grotesque or the overtly terrifying. It's about the subtle terror that creeps up on you, the kind that makes your skin crawl without even knowing why. It's the quiet whisper in a silent room, the faint rustling sound in an empty house, the fleeting shadow that seems to dart just out of view.

These stories grip us not by showing us a monster, but by making us imagine it in the darkest corners of our own minds. Once again, classics like Shirley Jackson's *The Haunting of Hill House* or more contemporary examples like Paul Tremblay's *A Head Full of Ghosts* excel in this. They weave a web of suspense without the need for graphic horror. Instead, they create an immersive atmosphere where the reader is compelled to look over their shoulder, question the creaks and groans of their own house, and doubt the reliability of their senses.

In psychological horror, the real horror is the possibility, the 'what if,' the unexplored and unexplained. It's the fear of the unknown, the dread of what might be hiding in the shadows of our own psyche. As you write, remember that the most powerful element of fear is often not the monster that is seen, but the one that resides in our imagination, unseen and waiting.

Crafting Your Own Psychological Terror

When you're weaving your own tapestry of psychological horror, think of yourself as a chef carefully selecting ingredients to create a dish that lingers in the mind long after it's consumed. The key ingredients? Atmosphere, insight into the human psyche, and a mastery of suspense.

- Focus on Atmosphere: Your setting isn't just a backdrop. It's an active participant in your story. An old house with creaking floorboards, a deserted street bathed in the cold glow of a lone streetlamp, an eerie forest where the trees seem to whisper secrets. These are more than locations. They are entities that set the tone of your narrative. Use these settings to craft an environment that breathes with foreboding, one that sets the stage for the psychological drama to unfold.

- Dive into the Human Psyche: The most haunting horrors are those that reside within us. Explore the fears, guilt, anxieties, and desires of your characters. What are they afraid to face? What secrets lie buried in their past? The real terror often lies not in external threats, but in the shadows of our own minds. By delving into these psychological depths, you create characters that are not only relatable but also deeply flawed and fascinatingly complex. This exploration makes the horror personal and, therefore, much more terrifying.

- Build Suspense Gradually: Think of suspense as a slow, simmering flame that gradually intensifies. A sudden shock can startle, but a carefully built tension that grows with each page is what truly unnerves the reader. Plant seeds of doubt, leave clues that only half-reveal the truth, and let the reader's imagination fill in the gaps. The fear of what might happen can often be more petrifying than the event itself. Let the anticipation of the unknown build, and when the climax arrives, it will be all the more impactful for the wait.

By focusing on these elements, you can create a story that doesn't just scare, but haunts the reader's thoughts long after they've turned the last page. Remember, in psychological horror, the unseen and the unspoken hold the real power.

The Role of Gore in Horror

As we pivot to the more visceral facet of horror, we enter the realm of gore. Gore in horror is as straightforward as it gets—it's the tangible, the explicit, the in-your-face shock value. Picture the severed limbs in *The Evil Dead*, the relentless, heart-pounding chases of *Halloween*, or the grotesque, skin-crawling transformations in *The Thing*. These aren't just scenes. They are visceral experiences that evoke a physical reaction from the audience.

But here's the thing about gore: it's a powerful tool in a writer's arsenal, much like a potent spice in a chef's kitchen. It needs to be used judiciously. Too much gore can desensitize your readers, making the horror feel overdone and losing its impact. On the other hand, if used sparingly or without conviction, your story may come off as half-hearted or lacking in intensity.

The key is to find that sweet spot where the use of gore enhances the emotional and psychological impact of your story. It should serve a purpose, whether it's to shock, to emphasize the gravity of a situation, or to make a statement about the fragility and vulnerability of the human body. When done right, gore can elevate a horror story, making it unforgettable. It can be a gut punch that leaves the reader reeling, but it's essential to remember that it should be part of a larger narrative tapestry. Gore for gore's sake can turn a story into a one-note symphony of shock, but when interwoven with strong character development, plot, and atmosphere, it can add a layer of intensity and realism to your tale.

So, as you paint your scenes with the brush of gore, ask yourself: does this add to my story's atmosphere, theme, or character development? Is it essential for the narrative, or is it merely decorative (decorative can be great if you're killing of a disliked character or villain)? The effective use of gore requires a delicate balance, but when struck, it can turn a good horror story into a visceral, unforgettable experience.

Finding the Right Amount of Gore

Determining the perfect measure of gore in your horror story is akin to a tightrope walk. It requires a keen sense of balance and a deep understanding of your audience (don't worry, this comes with time and experience). Not all readers are created equal in their tolerance or appreciation for gore. Some relish the visceral thrill that comes from explicit, blood-soaked scenes, while others may prefer a more subdued approach, finding too much graphic content off-putting or distracting. As a writer, it's crucial to gauge who your target audience is and tailor the level of gore in your story accordingly. This doesn't mean you should compromise your vision, but rather be mindful of who is likely to pick up your book.

When integrating gore into your narrative, always use it with a clear purpose. Gore for the sake of gore can come off as gratuitous and may cheapen the impact of your story. I tend to laugh out loud when a scene is more comical than horror. Instead, utilize it to amplify the stakes, deepen the plot, or reveal critical aspects of your characters. For instance, a sudden, gory scene can underscore a character's descent into madness or the brutality of the antagonist.

Moreover, balance is absolutely key in the use of gore. A story that relentlessly bombards the reader with graphic content can become numbing and lose its emotional impact. On the other hand, interspersing moments of gore with suspenseful build-ups or quieter, reflective scenes can create a more impactful and dynamic narrative. This rhythm allows readers to catch their breath, process what they've read, and build anticipation for what's to come. It immediately forces them to care about your protagonist even more. It's this ebb and flow, the contrast between the shocking and the subtle, that can turn a horror story into a compelling, multi-faceted experience that resonates with a wide range of readers. Remember, the right amount of gore can make your horror story a gripping and memorable journey, but finding that sweet spot is a craft in itself.

Merging Psychological Horror and Gore

In the intricate world of horror writing, the most unforgettable stories are often those that masterfully blend psychological terror with elements of gore. This fusion is a delicate balancing act, one that creates a deeply unsettling experience by simultaneously attacking both the mind and the senses of the reader.

Envision this combination as a carefully choreographed dance. At times, psychological horror takes the lead, guiding the reader through a maze of uncertainty, anxiety, and suspense. It's about crafting an atmosphere so tense that the reader's own imagination begins to conjure up fears far beyond what's on the page. This type of horror plays on anticipation, on the dread of what's lurking in the dark corners of the narrative (and the reader's mind).

Then, at just the right moment, when the reader is teetering on the edge of this psychological precipice, gore enters the stage. It arrives with a visceral force, a sudden and shocking burst of reality that anchors the hazy fears in a tangible, often blood-soaked form. This stark contrast can heighten the overall impact of the story, giving the abstract fears a concrete form.

The key to this dance is knowing when to shift between the two. The psychological elements set the stage, creating an immersive environment ripe with potential horrors, while the gore delivers the physical manifestation of these terrors. It's a push and pull that, when done correctly, can leave a lasting impression on the reader. The transition should feel natural, almost inevitable, and serve to enhance the narrative rather than distract from it.

By skillfully merging psychological horror with elements of gore, you create a multi-layered experience that resonates on multiple levels. It's not just about shocking the reader; it's about crafting a story that haunts them, that lingers in their thoughts long after the last page is turned. In the end, the most effective horror stories are those that can seamlessly navigate this intricate dance between the mind and the visceral, leaving the reader both intellectually and emotionally stirred.

Tips for Blending the Two:

- Begin by crafting an atmosphere thick with suspense. This approach leverages the power of suggestion, allowing readers' imaginations to conjure up their own personalized fears. By setting a scene that whispers of unseen dangers, you invite readers to project their deepest anxieties onto the narrative. It's about making the unknown a canvas for the mind, where every shadow or unexplained sound adds to a growing sense of dread. This method lays the groundwork for a more profound impact when the physical elements of horror are finally introduced.

- Gore should be used strategically, like a punctuation mark that accentuates key points in your story. When you introduce gore at crucial moments, it acts as a jolt to the narrative, shocking readers and adding intensity to the plot. As I mentioned before, this isn't about gratuitous violence. It's about using gore as a tool to heighten the stakes and deepen the emotional response. By timing these moments carefully, you ensure they contribute meaningfully to the story's progression, delivering a powerful impact that resonates with the reader.

- A successful horror story often lies in its rhythm—a dance of tension and release, of implied threats and overt horrors. By varying the tempo, alternating between the subtle chill of psychological horror and the stark brutality of gore, you keep your readers engaged and on edge. This unpredictability is key. It ensures that your audience remains invested in the story, uncertain of what lies around the next corner. It's about striking a balance between the seen and unseen, the said and unsaid, keeping readers in a constant state of anticipation and suspense.

Whether you choose to delve into the depths of the human psyche or paint the pages with gory details, remember this: horror, in any form, is about evoking emotion. It's about making the heart race and the mind whirl. So, as you pen down those eerie scenes and blood-curdling moments, ask yourself, "What would scare me? What would keep me up at night?"

Chapter 2

The Art of Subtext in Horror

As we venture deeper into the realm of advanced horror writing techniques, let's explore a tool that can transform your stories from mere tales of terror into profound reflections on the human condition: subtext. Subtext is the underlying layer of meaning, the unspoken undercurrent that runs beneath the surface narrative. It's what gives your story depth, turning it into a multi-dimensional piece that resonates with readers on various levels.

Understanding Subtext in Horror

Subtext in horror is akin to the unexplored depths of a haunted mansion: on the surface, you have your engaging story, the rooms and hallways where the action unfolds. But the real intrigue lies in the hidden passages and secret rooms—the themes, symbols, and metaphors that give your story its depth and complexity. These are the layers beneath the surface narrative that invite your readers to delve deeper, to think and feel beyond the immediate frights.

Imagine your narrative as this intriguing mansion. The story you tell is the path through its corridors, but the subtext—all those underlying ideas—is like uncovering hidden nooks and crannies packed with untold secrets. Here lies the opportunity to engage with broader concepts: our innermost fears, the psychological battles we face, or the big moral questions that don't always have clear answers. It's this blend of thrilling horror with thought-provoking themes that leaves a lasting impression on your readers.

Remember what Alfred Hitchcock, the master of suspense, once said: "Subtext is like baking a cake. The better the ingredients, the richer the cake. It's what's underneath that makes the story compelling." This analogy highlights the essence of subtext in storytelling. Like a well-baked cake, a story's appeal isn't just in its overt scares, but also in the richness of its hidden layers. As you craft your horror tale, think about these unseen elements. They are the key to transforming a simple spooky story into a profound narrative that resonates on a deeper level, captivating and lingering in the minds of your readers long after the thrill of the scare has passed. Subtext is also one of the main things a good reviewer will focus on.

Crafting Effective Subtext

- Choose Your Themes Wisely: The first step in embedding subtext into your horror story is to thoughtfully select the themes or underlying messages you wish to explore. These themes can be as broad as societal critiques, like the perils of consumerism or the tragic consequences of environmental neglect, or as intimate as personal struggles with loss, identity, addiction, or the fear of the unknown. The art lies in the subtlety of their integration. These themes should weave through your narrative like threads in a tapestry, enriching the story without dominating it. They are the undercurrents that give depth to the plot and characters, inviting readers to look beyond the surface scares to find the hidden meanings that resonate on a deeper, more intellectual level.

- Use Symbols and Metaphors: In the realm of horror, symbolism and metaphor are your allies in crafting a rich subtext. By infusing objects, characters, or even settings with symbolic meaning, you add layers to your story that resonate beyond the immediate narrative. A house in decay, for instance, could be more than a setting. It might reflect the crumbling mental state of a character, or the disintegration of a family. Similarly, a persistent fog shrouding a town isn't just an atmospheric touch. It could symbolize the cloud of uncertainty and confusion that permeates the mystery at hand. These symbols and metaphors serve as bridges, connecting the surface story to deeper themes and ideas, allowing readers to uncover hidden depths and meanings as they journey through your tale. The key is to weave these elements subtly into your narrative, allowing them to emerge naturally, enriching the story and engaging the reader's imagination and interpretive skills.

• Character Actions and Dialogue: In the realm of subtext, your characters are more than just players in your story. They are the vessels through which deeper themes are conveyed. Every action they take, every choice they make, and every word they utter can be imbued with additional layers of meaning. Pay close attention to their interactions and the nuances of their speech. What they openly express and, perhaps more importantly, what they leave unsaid can be powerful indicators of the underlying themes you're exploring. Picture a former addict protagonist, deep into the second act of your book and on the verge of giving up, driving by a pharmacy or liquor store. You don't have to dive into his/her thoughts. Merely looking at the building and squeezing their eyes shut or clenching the steering wheel can say so much more.

These subtleties can reveal hidden fears, unspoken desires, or internal conflicts, enriching the narrative with a complexity that invites readers to look beyond the surface and ponder the deeper significance of each character's journey.

Example of Subtext in Horror

The rain batters the windows of the old Anderson house. Emily stands in the dimly lit kitchen, staring at the flickering candle on the table. The walls, once vibrant with life, now peeled with neglect, mirror the turmoil inside her.

Her brother, Michael, sits across from her, his eyes hollow, a shadow of the boy who once filled the house with laughter. "Do you think we'll ever make it out of here alive?" His voice barely rises above the storm outside.

Emily hesitates, her gaze drifting to the darkened hallway. "And go where?" she replies, her voice tinged with a weariness that goes beyond sleepless nights. "This house, it's all we have left of them. We have to save it."

Michael's gaze follows hers, resting on the portrait at the end of the hall—their parents, smiling, a stark contrast to the gloom that now envelopes the house. "But it's eating us alive, Em. It's this damn house!"

Emily turns away, her eyes brimming with unshed tears. "Perhaps we should die here," she whispers, the candlelight casting long shadows that seem to dance mockingly on the walls.

The storm rages on. The house creaks and groans as if resonating with their sorrow. In its every corner, memories lurk, a constant reminder of what they lost.

In this scene, the old Anderson house serves as the monster and a symbol of the characters' emotional state. Its decaying walls and darkened hallways reflect Emily and Michael's grief and inability to move on from their parents' death. The storm outside mirrors the turmoil they feel inside, while the conversation subtly reveals their internal conflict between the desire to escape their pain and the fear of letting go. The scene is layered with subtext about grief, loss, and the psychological impact of holding onto the past.

Why Subtext Matters

Subtext adds layers to your story, making it a richer and more engaging experience. It invites readers to delve deeper, to think and ponder, turning your horror tale into something that lingers in their minds long after the last page is turned. It also allows your story to transcend the confines of the genre, making it not just a horror story, but a commentary on something larger, something more universally human.

Chapter 3

Metafiction and Self-Referential Horror

In the labyrinthine world of horror writing, there exists a path less traveled, yet immensely intriguing—the path of metafiction. Metafiction, in its simplest form, is a story that knows it's a story. It's a narrative that self-consciously reflects upon its own nature as a work of fiction, directly engaging with the reader and acknowledging its status as a construct of the imagination. In horror, this technique can add an exhilarating layer of depth, turning the story into a playground where reality and fiction blur, and where the reader becomes an active participant in the tale.

Understanding Metafiction in Horror

Envision a story that not only terrifies but also playfully engages its audience, one that cleverly manipulates and even comments on the traditional conventions of the genre. This is the essence of metafiction in horror. It's a self-aware narrative, one that might cheekily remark on its own unfolding plot, dissect its structure, or openly toy with the well-worn tropes of horror itself. This approach establishes a conversation with the reader, inviting them into a deeper dialogue about the story they are experiencing. Metafiction does more than just tell a tale. It questions and explores the very nature of fear and storytelling.

It blurs the line between fiction and reality, encouraging readers to ponder where one ends and the other begins. This unique form of engagement elevates the reading experience, transforming it into an interactive exploration of the mechanisms of horror and the psychology behind why we are drawn to tales that send shivers down our spine.

Techniques for Crafting Metafictional Horror

- Breaking the Fourth Wall: This involves the story or characters directly addressing the reader, making them aware that they're engaging with a work of fiction. It's like a nod and a wink, a moment where the narrative acknowledges its own ploy. Imagine a scene in a horror novel where the protagonist suddenly turns to the reader and says, "You might be wondering why I'm heading into this obviously haunted house. Well, if I didn't, there wouldn't be much of a story, would there?" This direct address acknowledges the reader's presence and the fictional nature of the story. *House of Leaves* by Mark Z. Danielewski is a complex novel that often breaks the fourth wall, challenging the reader's perception of text and story.

- Playing with Horror Tropes: Use the story to comment on or subvert common horror tropes. This could be done through characters discussing the clichés of horror or by the narrative structure itself challenging the traditional rules of the genre. I'll always remember the movie *Scream* as my first introduction to this type of metafiction. In a story, it's as simple as a character saying, "We shouldn't split up, that's exactly what every horror movie character does before they get killed." This self-aware dialogue plays with the reader's expectations and knowledge of horror clichés.

- Story within a Story: Embed a secondary narrative that mirrors or comments on the main story. This can create a sense of depth and complexity, as the reader navigates multiple layers of fiction. A novel could feature a character reading a book, and the plot of that book eerily starts to reflect and comment on the events of the main narrative, creating a mirrored story layer. *Night Film* by Marisha Pessl incorporates a variety of multimedia elements and a secondary narrative that complements the primary story, adding layers of mystery and complexity.

- Authorial Intrusion: Introduce the author's voice directly into the story, either as a narrator or a character. This can be a powerful tool for adding commentary or guiding the reader's interpretation. As the author, you might insert a personal footnote in the narrative, such as, "At this point in the story, I struggled with how my character should react. In the real world, no one would be brave enough to do what I'm about to write." Just ensure that it builds on the suspense and intrigue. Don't break the reader's suspended disbelief. *S.* by J.J. Abrams and Doug Dorst includes notes and marginalia within the text, providing commentary and insights that directly involve the authors' perspectives.

The Power of Metafiction in Horror

Metafiction in horror does more than just entertain. It invites the reader to engage with the story on a cerebral level. It's a method that can add humor, deepen thematic exploration, and challenge the reader's perception of reality. By acknowledging its own fictionality, a horror story can highlight the artificiality of its scares, and in a complete paradox, make them feel more real and immediate.

In a way, metafictional horror is like a haunted house that knows it's a haunted house and isn't afraid to tell you. It plays with your expectations, leading you down familiar corridors only to reveal hidden doors and secret passageways you never knew existed. It's a journey that reminds you of the thrill of being scared while simultaneously making you question why you enjoy the sensation in the first place.

As you tread the path of horror writing, consider the allure of metafiction. It's a journey that promises to be as rewarding as it is unsettling, a dance on the tightrope between illusion and reality.

Chapter 4

Sensory Writing and Immersive Experiences

Welcome to the next step in our journey through the advanced techniques of horror writing. In this chapter, we'll delve into the art of sensory writing and how it can be used to create immersive and visceral experiences for your readers. Sensory writing is about engaging not just the mind, but the body of the reader, by evoking the five senses – sight, sound, smell, taste, and touch. When done well, it can transport readers directly into the heart of your horror story, making them feel as though they're living the terror alongside your characters.

While sensory details should consistently be there to enrich your narrative, there are pivotal scenes where this technique can be particularly impactful. These are the moments where you can afford to slow down the pace, narrowing the lens tightly on your character's point of view. In these scenes, delve deeply into the sensory experiences, painting every sight, sound, smell, taste, and touch with meticulous care. It's like bringing a magnifying glass to the moment, heightening the reader's immersion and emotional connection. Whether it's the tense stillness before a horrifying revelation, the disorienting confusion of a supernatural encounter, or the intimate terror of a character facing their deepest fear, these scenes are your opportunity to fully engage the reader's senses. Make time stand still!

By slowing down and focusing intensely on sensory details, you transform these moments into a rich tapestry of experience, making them not just readable, but palpable and hauntingly memorable.

Engaging the Five Senses

- Sight: Visual descriptions are fundamental in horror. Paint a vivid picture of the setting, the characters, and the unfolding events. Use color, light, and shadow to create mood and atmosphere. Describe the eerie glow of a ghostly apparition or the stark, blood-red stain on an otherwise pristine wall.

- Sound: Sound can be incredibly effective in building tension. The creak of a floorboard, the rustling of leaves, a distant, indistinct whisper—these can all set the reader's nerves on edge. Pay attention to the rhythm and cadence of your words as they can mimic the sounds within the story.

- Smell: Smells can evoke strong emotional reactions. The mustiness of an old house, the iron tang of blood, or the sickly-sweet odor of decay can all create a visceral response and add realism to your scenes.

- Taste: Though less commonly used in horror, taste can be a powerful tool. The metallic taste of fear, the bitterness of a potion, or the ashen taste of smoke from a mysterious fire can be very evocative.

- Touch: Conveying texture and physical sensation can draw readers deeper into your story. The prickle of fear on the back of the neck, the clamminess of cold sweat, or the roughness of ancient stone under fingertips can all enhance the sense of immersion.

Creating Immersive Experiences

- Show, Don't Tell: Bring scenes to life by showing the fear through your character's senses. Instead of stating, "The room was scary," describe the chill creeping up the character's spine, the eerie creak of the floorboards, and the ghostly flicker of shadows on the wall. Let the reader feel the character's heartbeat quicken and their breath catch in a throat gripped by fear.

- Use Active Language: Active language makes your descriptions more vivid and engaging. Compare the passive "It was windy" with "The wind howled fiercely, piercing through the cracks with a banshee's wail." The latter paints a vivid picture, placing the reader right in the heart of the scene, feeling the wind's raw power and hearing its haunting cry.

- Varying Sensory Details: Balance is key in sensory writing. Focus on different senses to create a well-rounded experience. If a scene heavily emphasizes visual details, consider adding auditory, olfactory, or tactile elements. This prevents sensory overload and keeps the reader grounded in the character's experience, making the narrative more relatable and vivid.

- Create Contrast: Use contrast to amplify the horror. After describing an intense, loud scene—perhaps a cacophony of screams and crashes – follow it with eerie, suffocating silence. This stark contrast can be more unnerving than the initial chaos, playing on the reader's anticipation and fear of the unknown. It's the quiet that follows the storm that often holds the most terror.

The Power of Sensory Writing in Horror

Sensory writing in horror isn't just about providing a laundry list of sensory details. It's about choosing the right details at the right time to evoke specific emotions and reactions. By engaging the reader's senses, you invite them not just to read your story, but to experience it. The ultimate goal is to create a world so vivid and tangible that the reader feels transported into the heart of the horror, experiencing every chill, every whisper, every shadow as if they were right there. This is the essence of creating a truly immersive horror experience.

Section 2

Setting & Atmosphere

Welcome to the part of horror writing where setting isn't just the background of your story, it's one of the main characters. Think of it as the perfect haunted house, where every creak and groan tells a part of the story, setting the tone and shaping the mood right from the get-go. It's not just where your story happens. It's a key player that can reflect what's going on inside your characters.

Then there's atmosphere—that hard-to-pin-down feeling that makes your spine tingle even before anything scary happens. It's what turns a regular old graveyard from a sad place into the kind of spot you wouldn't want to visit after dark. Without the right atmosphere, the scariest scenes might not even raise a goosebump. So, let's dive in and figure out how to make your setting and atmosphere work hard to give your readers the chills they're craving.

Chapter 1

The Art of World-Building

In the rich landscape of storytelling, genres like horror, fantasy, and science fiction hold a special place, inviting readers into worlds veiled in shadow and mystery. The magic of these tales often lies in the craft of world-building—the careful construction of settings that are not just backdrops but living, breathing entities in their own right. These worlds, be they dark forests shrouded in fog, dystopian futures, or realms woven from pure imagination, pulse with their own set of rules, myths, and hidden dangers.

- Foundations of Fear and Fantasy: In the realm of horror, the foundation of every world lies in a delicate balance between the every day and the extraordinary, the familiar and the utterly terrifying. It's about crafting a set of rules that govern everything from the eerie flicker of candlelight to the monstrous entities lurking in the dark, creating a reality where the ordinary can suddenly twist into the domain of nightmares, making every shadow a potential threat and every silence a precursor to screams.

- Cultures Cloaked in Darkness: The most unforgettable horror settings are draped in cultures woven from the threads of superstition, ritual, and dark legend. These cultural backdrops do more than just decorate the narrative—they infuse it with a palpable sense of dread and anticipation, painting the lives of their inhabitants with broad strokes of fear and a constant tension that pulses through the very air they breathe.

- Whispers from the Beyond: The history of a horror world is often a tapestry of chilling tales, ancient curses, and tragedies that refuse to be forgotten. These stories from the past don't just add layers of intrigue, though. They seep into the present, haunting the living spaces and influencing the current narrative, turning the setting itself into a storyteller that whispers secrets of days long gone yet never truly laid to rest.

- Terrains That Tremble: Every horror story is deeply rooted in its setting, with landscapes that do more than set the scene—they evoke a visceral response. Be it the oppressive gloom of fog-laden moors, the eerie silence of abandoned places, or the suffocating closeness of dimly lit corridors, these terrains are active elements that shape the story's mood and push characters to their limits. Rely on the readers' past experiences with these terrains to strengthen your story

- The Currency of Fear: In the shadowy corners of horror worlds, the economy isn't just about the exchange of goods but also the trade in darker currencies: secrets, power, and survival. This underlying economy adds a tangible layer of realism and desperation, painting a complex picture of societal dynamics where fear and desire drive characters to acts of bravery or betrayal.

- Mysticism in the Shadows: The supernatural forces at play in horror worlds, from arcane rituals to ghostly apparitions, are bound by their own mysterious rules. These elements bring a sense of wonder and danger, challenging characters to navigate a world where magic is as real as the darkness and every spell comes with a price.

- Creatures in the Dark: Horror worlds are often populated with beings that defy the laws of nature, embodying the unknown and the feared. These creatures, from spectral entities to unspeakable monsters, serve as both adversaries and symbols of the world's enigmatic core, challenging characters and readers alike to confront the primal fears that lurk in the dark.

- Intrigues and Infernos: The political and social conflicts that simmer in the heart of horror settings reflect a complex web of ambitions, fears, and alliances. These struggles for power and control mirror the unpredictability of human nature, adding a layer of tension and drama that complements the supernatural elements, making the world feel fully realized and dangerously alive.

- Ethical Quandaries and Moral Mazes: The ethical landscape in horror is often a murky terrain, where right and wrong blur into shades of grey. Characters find themselves at crossroads that test their values and morality, forcing them, and the reader, to navigate a maze of difficult choices that challenge preconceived notions of justice, loyalty, and humanity.

World-building in horror, fantasy, and science fiction is a delicate balance between the known and the unknown, between the light of imagination and the dark of fear. It's about crafting worlds that breathe with their own life, that invite readers in and then haunt them long after the last page is turned. A well-built world is a gateway to the unknown, offering endless paths to explore, mysteries to uncover, and, ultimately, a journey that feels as real as it is fantastical. A well-established world is also vital for the start of a well-loved series.

Chapter 2

Set and Setting - Ben Eads

Let's talk about where your story takes place, shall we? How big of a role does it play in modern fiction—short and long? That depends on your story. What's the plot? What character arcs do you have? We could go on and on, but where your story takes place will in some way interact with most, if not all of these. It's like a thread woven through a quilt, and the more alive your set and setting, the more alive your story, be it short or long. What time of year is it? Utilizing characters' senses helps us feel at home. If it's summer, Honeysuckle may carry on the air. And myriad other flora. Whatever you choose needs to count. In winter? Dead leaves and freshly fallen snow. Does the story take place in the USA? Or the UK? Or South Africa?

Whether you're a pantser or a plotter, set and setting are comprised of description, narration, Deep POV, and time. The shorter the narrative, the less set and setting. Set is the character's emotional temperature around their space, their home, apartment, and other people. Do others raise or lower the character's emotional temperature? Can the emotional state be likened to the weather? Or actually tied to the weather itself, in a supernatural phenomenon? Or insert whatever supernatural element. Is your character falling apart like their world? We would want to care for or find the city or town interesting, as well. Or wherever your story takes place. Again, we need to feel at home. A home that has been constructed of things that move the story forward. They can also be layered in. Deep POV and effective narration are just two examples, just off the top of my head.

Wherever your story takes place, it needs to feel lived in. Regardless of your word count, wherever your story takes place needs to feel lived in. I cannot stress this enough. Think of The Last of Us, or True Detective, and you can see how set and setting weaves its way throughout. Any story, really. In The Last of Us, it either impedes them, helps them, or turns their adventure on a dime. In True Detective, we see set and setting weaved throughout the story nicely. Joe R. Lansdale's stories always have a lived-in feel. Welcome to Muddy Creek, Texas!

Which brings us to description, as it relates only to the story for setting. You've seen it. You created it. You know it so well. You've read the smelly thing forty-six times, and you would like to put it away. The reader does not know any of this. Sure, you can overdo description, just as you can underdo it. But you could also slap the reader with details that don't matter or underperform. Create a place for your reader to experience all the sights, sounds, and smells. Don't forget about smells. Stephen King said: "Description begins with the writer and ends with the reader." Another way of saying the same thing, or, perhaps, going deeper, is interacting with the reader on a subconscious level. If your protagonist answers their front door, and you write: The kid wore baggy jeans, a Slayer T-shirt, and chains hung from his pockets, then you're eliciting a reaction in the reader's subconscious. They are painting the picture with you. Some will think this young man is bad news. But did you get the chains hanging from his pockets? Note well how I didn't go into a description of his chains, but it had the effect of letting a reader make their mind up about this unwelcome visitor.

Where your character lives—be it a shitty apartment with a leaky shower devoured by black mold—needs to be real for us. Keep asking yourself if it serves the story. Will we see this again later in the story? Again, we're weaving that quilt, and making sure it's sound and beautiful, in its own dark way. Don't show them the movie that you've seen in your head for so long, whilst writing and revising. Show them paintings of the scenes your imagination conjured. Only years of writing will hone those skills. The above example also creates suspense in a stealthy way.

Editors of the press you submit your stories to receive an enormous amount of fiction, whether it's an open call for novels and novellas, or short fiction for an anthology. We know a lot about your submissions by reading the first paragraph. When you're weaving your story together, whether the second or third draft, remember that you, the author of the story, know this place better than anyone. You have authority. You see it so clearly in your mind, you're able to construct this really cool story. Use it. Weave that thread! Bringing this out will greatly enhance your chances of acceptance. I cannot stress how important this is. Whether it's the short story itself, "Children of the Corn," or IT, we see how a master of horror weaves it all together. Remember that little, vacant town with a church, a parked car, and a cornfield? In IT, due to it being a long novel, without the people, and the hate people have in their hearts for others in myriad form, the layout of the city itself, and its catacombs—without any of these, Pennywise would go somewhere else. He feeds off of this. The barrens await! And note well how when they built the dam, it was a moment that bonded them for life. It also had consequences for Derry's River and water works. And some bad stuff happened there, too. Some really bad stuff. A lot of really bad stuff. Just as unknowing and labyrinthine is Derry's water-works, so is the adventure itself.

The more lived in your story feels, the more we feel as if we're the main characters, experiencing a world we know so well. It's like sitting in your favorite chair; as soon as you do, you know it's just right, and it has all the memory of what has occurred in that house or apartment or flat. If you write a line saying: "Harvey poured what was left of the milk from his cereal back into the container. He looked out the window at the desperate city." Then we can start to fall into your story. I want to know more about this.

Don't overthink it. Look for this in your first, second, or third drafts and decide how much cozier you can make the reader feel. This is where effective narration and Deep POV come in, whether you're writing in first or third person. Let us feel the world through your character. How do they size their lives up, and their current situation? What casts a shadow on them still? Strive to show, as opposed to tell, with effective narration and internal thoughts. Not that telling is bad. In fact, you'll find a mashup of showing and telling in a paragraph...but not all the time. Use Deep POV to show us through action, body language, dialogue, or internal thoughts, where your character is when we start reading your story. Or the lay of the land. If you grab us, then your story will be read. Most stories that hopeful authors have submitted don't make it past the first few paragraphs. As editors, we're looking for a lot more than just set and setting, but, again, so much depends upon it. Again, the how much or how little depends on the story. Remember: the story is the boss. If you find it fighting you and not wanting to comply with what you think will really enhance the set and setting of your story, stop. It's the story telling you: Nope! Obey the story.

I accepted a short story by an amazing writer, Jennifer Loring, for Tales from The Lake: Volume 4. Here, we have tragedy of the worst kind. Where it happens is in a small house with a small backyard. The small above-ground pool plays a large role in this small backyard. A traumatic event happened here, and Loring knows how to interact with the reader's subconscious. And that's what we want to feel as readers, but, more importantly, editors. Loring fits everything together like Legos.

When I was writing my horror novella Cracked Sky, published by Crystal Lake Entertainment, I understood, right from the first sentence, that this harrowing story and journey through the ultimate loss was fraught with horrible weather that ceased to rain, for weeks. Rusted buildings are here and there. It just came to me naturally, and at the time, I didn't know why. But I did know, right from the first, it was an emotional story that required it. Despite the story taking place in Florida, the foliage doesn't look so green to my main character, Stephen. Stephen and his wife have just lost their six-year-old daughter in a car accident. When Stephen was sitting on his back porch, smoking a cigarette, I wrote what you would hear when I'm sitting on my back porch, here in Central Florida. The rain hitting his roof and pack porch, too. A lot of rain. As Stephen became stronger, more resourceful, or reckless, the saw palmettos and palms looked green and bright. This is also a way of showing the reader something. If I had come out and said: Stephen was feeling happier that day, it's a washout. A whoopsie!

And if you self-publish, everything we've discussed still applies. I would caution self-published authors to always, always, use a professional editor to edit their work. If they can afford it, of course. It's hard times for everyone right now. Which reminds me of a joke: Gary comes home from quitting work and his neighbor waves.

"How's it going, Gary?"

"I'm a writer now!"

"That's great, Gary. Have you sold anything?"

"Yeah! My house, my car."

The plight of a writer! But even if you're submitting to a press with a kick-ass editor, I would advise using amazing beta readers or a professional editor. It makes all the difference.

Time itself can be part of set and setting. I'll use some examples almost everyone has read. With Jack Ketchum's The Girl Next Door, we see a very small neighborhood and, more importantly, its history, its time. We also see the now, the societal concerns. Gossip carries on the wind. Socioeconomics defines the characters' lives in so many ways. It's a deep, harrowing novel—an examination of human beings' behavior when confronted with the darkest evil. And each step of the way, you're watching set and setting being used masterfully, and gracefully. You're witness to everything this little boy sees. And feels. Hard to pull that off. Ketchum makes the neighborhood a character.

Stephen King's novel Salem's Lot is actually about the town. Sure, there are vampires and characters which populate the town, but the first character we're introduced to is Salem's Lot itself. The Marston house—and its sordid history—sits atop a hill that's seen a lot of death. An unspeakable act occurred there, too. And something worse just arrived in town. Each character shows you their own unique perspective of Salem's Lot as the story is moving forward. Or, more importantly, what they're trying to forget about it.

Bradbury's The October Country relies heavily on set and setting. Not all of those amazing short stories do, but it's a great example to show how set and setting differ from story to story. Same goes for any story. Using effective description, narration, deep Pov, and time, will help the reader feel at home. Cozy, even. Here's some hot chocolate. Again, you know more about the world you created than anyone else. When you're drafting your story down—short or long—make sure you've made it interactive. It's the deft hand that interacts with the reader's imagination. Make them feel at home.

Ben's short fiction has appeared in magazines or anthologies by Crystal Lake Entertainment, Shroud Magazine, Corpus Press, and Seventh Star Press. His horror novellas, Cracked Sky, and Hollow Heart are now available from the Bram Stoker Award ® Winning press, Crystal Lake Entertainment.

Chapter 3

How Setting Amplifies Thematic Undertones

In the intricate dance of storytelling, setting and theme are partners, moving in tandem to create a narrative experience that resonates. While the setting provides the physical and cultural landscape of the story, the theme offers its deeper, often universal, message or insight. When these two elements align and resonate, the setting becomes more than just a backdrop—it becomes a reflection and amplifier of the story's thematic undertones. Here's how setting can resonate with and enhance thematic depth:

Reflecting Inner Landscapes

The settings in horror can serve as a tangible reflection of a character's inner turmoil or journey. Imagine a protagonist navigating a fog-enshrouded forest, each step forward mirroring their struggle through a haze of confusion or grief. Or picture an abandoned house, its crumbling walls and shattered windows echoing the character's fractured psyche. These environments do more than set the scene. They embody the character's emotional state, making the intangible anguish, fear, or hope they experience something readers can almost touch and see, thus deepening the thematic resonance of the narrative.

Cultural and Societal Commentary

In the realm of horror, the societal structure and cultural backdrop of the setting can serve as a powerful lens for examining themes of control, conformity, and rebellion. Envision a town under the thumb of a pervasive cult, its every custom and law steeped in secrecy and fear, challenging characters (and readers) to confront the dangers of blind allegiance. Or consider a post-apocalyptic society where the remnants of humanity cling to draconian laws to maintain order, raising questions about the price of security and the human capacity for resilience and adaptation in the face of societal collapse.

Historical Echoes

Placing a horror story within a specific historical context can imbue the narrative with a rich layer of thematic depth. A tale set in the shadowy corridors of a Victorian asylum could explore the theme of enlightenment clashing with ignorance, mirroring the era's tumultuous relationship with mental health and science. Similarly, a story woven around an ancient, forgotten civilization might delve into themes of legacy, memory, and the inexorable passage of time, using the echoes of history to comment on the cyclical nature of human triumph and tragedy.

Nature's Lessons

Horror often taps into the primal forces of nature to explore profound thematic questions. A relentless storm battering a coastal town, indifferent to the plight of its inhabitants, might reflect on the theme of human insignificance in the face of nature's might, challenging characters to find meaning in resilience or surrender. Alternatively, a serene valley, untouched by time and human folly, could serve as a backdrop for a narrative about purity, innocence, and the corruptive influence of civilization, prompting reflections on the delicate balance between human progress and the sanctity of the natural world.

Symbolic Locations

In horror, locations steeped in symbolism can serve as powerful conduits for theme. A dilapidated church might stand as a stark reminder of lost faith or the corruption of sanctity, while an overgrown graveyard could whisper tales of forgotten lives and the inexorable march of time. I used to love visiting abandoned buildings and photographing the ruins (back when I still had free time on my hands). Abandoned schools, with their silent halls and empty classrooms, might evoke the loss of innocence or the harsh lessons learned outside of youth's idealism. Crossroads, shrouded in mist, can become a haunting metaphor for pivotal life decisions or the paths not taken, each direction laden with unseen consequences.

Juxtaposition and Contrast

The deliberate contrast of settings within a horror narrative can sharply illuminate thematic undercurrents. Imagine the stark disparity between the relentless pace of a neon-lit metropolis and the timeless rhythm of a neighboring village, where life flows as gently as the winding river. This contrast can vividly highlight the relentless march of progress and its impact on tradition, community, and the environment, inviting readers to ponder the true cost of modern life's conveniences and the value of harmony with nature.

Evolution and Transformation

Watching a setting undergo significant change can mirror the thematic evolution within the story. A vibrant community spiraling into desolation can serve as a poignant backdrop for exploring themes of loss, resilience, or the inevitable fade of glory days. Conversely, a blighted land slowly blooming back to life under the care of determined survivors can symbolize hope, renewal, and the powerful drive for rebirth in the aftermath of catastrophe, reflecting the human capacity for regeneration in the face of despair.

Challenges and Trials

The very landscape of a horror setting can be fraught with trials that test characters to their limits, embodying the thematic essence of struggle and survival. A treacherous mountain path, shrouded in storm clouds, might not just be a physical barrier but a metaphor for the internal battles fought by those who dare to traverse it, symbolizing the journey through personal storms and the quest for inner peace amidst turmoil. The relentless environment acts as both adversary and crucible, shaping characters through their confrontation with fear, uncertainty, and the raw elements, ultimately reflecting the indomitable resilience of the human spirit.

Think of *The Lord of the Rings* with Frodo and Sam's perilous journey through the rocky passes of the Emyn Muil and their subsequent ascent of the sheer cliffs of Cirith Ungol. These treacherous landscapes are not just physical obstacles. They symbolize the immense internal struggles the characters face. As Frodo and Sam navigate these daunting terrains, their journey mirrors their battle against despair, temptation, and the weight of their quest. The storm-shrouded mountains and cliffs become metaphors for the overwhelming challenges they must overcome, both from the external world and their internal doubts and fears. This harrowing passage through Middle-earth's most forbidding landscapes tests their resolve, loyalty, and courage, symbolizing the thematic core of endurance and the triumph of the spirit over seemingly insurmountable odds.

When setting and theme resonate, they create a symphony of meaning, each amplifying the other's significance. The setting becomes more than just a place—it becomes a thematic echo chamber, where every hill, building, and street corner reverberates with the story's deeper message. By crafting settings that resonate with thematic undertones, writers can create richer, more layered narratives.

Chapter 4

Setting's influence on pacing and conflict

Setting and the story pace

Ever notice how some stories feel like a roller coaster, while others are more like a leisurely stroll through a park? That's pacing in action. And guess what? The setting of your story plays a huge role in setting that pace. Let's break down how the environment can either put the pedal to the metal or give us some time to breathe and reflect.

1. Fast & Furious: Certain environments naturally lend themselves to high-octane action. Think bustling city streets, stormy seas, or a ticking time bomb scenario. The movie *Speed* definitely comes to mind.

Tips to Get the Heart Racing:
- Crowded Places: The cacophony and chaos of crowded settings, like a bustling marketplace or a cramped subway, naturally inject a sense of urgency into the narrative. The frenetic energy and potential for unexpected encounters in these spaces can accelerate the pacing, pushing characters toward swift decisions and actions.

- Unpredictable Elements: Nature's fury, manifested in a sudden tempest or a rampant forest fire, introduces an element of unpredictability that demands immediate response. Such environmental challenges can drastically quicken the story's pace as characters are forced to react swiftly to survive.

- Tight Spaces: The palpable tension of being cornered in tight spaces, such as the claustrophobic confines of a sinking ship or the precarious rubble of a collapsing building, inherently hastens the narrative rhythm. The immediate danger and limited options for escape can create a rapid escalation of conflict and decision-making.

2. Slow & Steady: On the flip side, some settings invite introspection and a slower pace. Imagine a quiet lakeside, a snow-covered village, or a long, empty road stretching ahead.

Tips for Those Deep Moments:
- Nature's Embrace: The soothing ambiance of nature, such as the melodic murmur of a babbling brook or the soft whisper of leaves dancing in the wind, naturally fosters moments of introspection and calm. These serene settings invite characters to pause, reflect, and connect with their inner thoughts, offering readers a chance to delve deeper into the narrative's emotional landscape.

- Nighttime Stillness: The tranquil solitude of night, under a canopy of stars, provides a meditative stage for characters to ponder life's mysteries and their own journeys. This peaceful stillness, away from the day's clamor, opens up a space for introspective dialogue and significant character revelations.

- Isolated Places: Settings like an untouched beach at dawn or a secluded cabin nestled in the forest offer a sanctuary from the world's noise, creating the perfect environment for contemplation. In these undisturbed locales, characters (and through them, the readers) find the mental and emotional room to explore deeper feelings and complex thoughts, enriching the narrative with profound insights.

3. Mixing It Up: A story that's all action or all reflection will feel one-dimensional. Mixing up settings can help vary the pace, keeping readers engaged.

Tips to Keep It Fresh:

- Transition Scenes: Transitioning between settings, such as the shift from the idyllic peace of a small village to the frenetic energy of a sprawling city, can dramatically alter the story's pace. This change in setting not only keeps readers engaged but also mirrors the characters' journey, adding a dynamic layer to the narrative as they adapt to new challenges and environments.

- Time of Day: The contrast in atmosphere from the vibrant hustle of a marketplace bathed in daylight to its serene, almost eerie quietude under the cloak of night can significantly influence the story's rhythm. This shift not only marks the passage of time but also adds depth to the setting, affecting the characters' actions and the overall mood of the narrative.

Think of your story's setting as the background music in a movie. It can either get your heart pumping with a fast beat or soothe you with a gentle melody. By being mindful of how the environment influences the story's rhythm, writers can craft narratives that resonate, engage, and captivate. So, next time you set the scene, consider the pace and let the environment set the tone.

How Environment Drives Conflict in Storytelling

The setting of a story is more than just a backdrop. It's a dynamic force that can instigate, escalate, and resolve conflicts. Whether it's the physical environment, the societal norms, or the historical context, the setting can introduce challenges and dilemmas that characters must navigate.

Here's a closer look at how setting can drive conflicts in a narrative:

Man vs. Nature: One of the most primal conflicts, this pits characters against the forces of nature. Whether it's a sailor battling a storm, a mountaineer facing the harsh conditions of a peak, or a community trying to survive a drought, the environment itself becomes the antagonist. The unpredictability and sheer power of nature can test characters' resilience, resourcefulness, and will to survive. Think of John Steinbeck's *The Grapes of Wrath*.

Cultural and Societal Norms: Every society has its rules, traditions, and expectations. When characters challenge or break these norms, conflict arises. This can be seen in stories about forbidden romances, rebellions against oppressive regimes, or individuals trying to break free from societal expectations.

Territorial Disputes: The setting can be a source of conflict when multiple parties lay claim to it. This could be two families feuding over a piece of land, nations going to war over territories, or tribes competing for control over hunting grounds.

Historical Tensions: The past events of a setting can sow the seeds of present conflicts. Old rivalries, historical injustices, or past betrayals can influence current events, leading to conflicts that have roots in the past.

Resource Scarcity: When resources are limited, competition intensifies. This can be seen in post-apocalyptic settings where survivors fight over dwindling supplies, or in stories set in overpopulated cities where space and resources are at a premium. Fingers crossed we don't find ourselves in this position some time soon.

Environmental Changes: Shifts in the environment, whether natural or man-made, can lead to conflict. This could be a community grappling with the effects of climate change, a city facing the challenges of rapid urbanization, or a village dealing with the aftermath of a natural disaster.

Clashes of Values: Different settings can have different values, beliefs, and worldviews. When characters from different backgrounds interact, their differing values can lead to misunderstandings, prejudices, and conflicts.

Entrapment and Isolation: Certain settings can trap characters, either physically or psychologically. This could be a remote island, a haunted mansion, or a dystopian society where escape seems impossible. The desire to break free can drive conflict, both internally (within a character's mind) and externally (against external forces or antagonists).

The setting is a crucible where conflicts are forged. It provides the challenges, dilemmas, and pressures that characters must face and overcome. By understanding the potential conflicts inherent in a setting, you can craft compelling narratives where the environment is not just a passive stage but an active force that shapes the story's trajectory.

Chapter 5

How Setting Influences Events in Storytelling

In the realm of storytelling, the setting is not just a passive backdrop against which events unfold. it actively shapes the narrative, influencing the trajectory of events and the choices characters make. The interplay between setting and plot is a dance of cause and effect, where the environment can act as both a catalyst and a constraint. Here's a deeper exploration of how setting can influence events in a story:

Natural Obstacles and Challenges

The physical landscape of a setting can present tangible challenges for characters. A treacherous mountain pass, a raging river, or a vast desert can become formidable obstacles that characters must navigate or overcome. Such challenges can drive the plot forward, forcing characters to devise solutions, make tough decisions, or confront their fears.

Once again, Tolkien's *The Lord of the Rings* is a great example. The Fellowship faces the daunting task of crossing the Misty Mountains. The treacherous conditions of Caradhras force them to reconsider their path, leading them to the perilous Mines of Moria. This choice is pivotal, directly impacting the group's dynamics and the story's direction, illustrating how natural obstacles can significantly influence a narrative's course.

Societal Norms and Constraints

Every setting has its own societal norms, laws, and cultural expectations. These can influence events by dictating what is acceptable or taboo. A character's rebellion against these norms, or their struggle to fit in, can be central to the narrative. For instance, a love story set in a society with strict class divisions might revolve around the challenges of a forbidden romance.

In Jane Austen's *Pride and Prejudice*, the societal norms and class divisions of Regency England play a crucial role. The romance between Elizabeth Bennet and Mr. Darcy is fraught with challenges due to their differing social standings, showcasing how societal expectations can shape personal relationships and drive the narrative forward.

Historical Context

The historical backdrop of a setting can shape events by providing context. A story set during a war will have events influenced by battles, political intrigue, and the broader conflict. Similarly, a tale set during an era of innovation might revolve around the advent of new technologies and the societal changes they bring.

Schindler's List by Thomas Keneally is set against the backdrop of World War II and the Holocaust, profoundly influencing the story's events. The historical context of the war and the atrocities committed during the Holocaust are central to the narrative, shaping the characters' decisions, actions, and fates.

Mood and Atmosphere

The atmosphere of a setting can influence the emotional tone of events. A gloomy, rain-soaked city might lend a sense of melancholy to a scene, while a bright, sunlit meadow could infuse a moment with joy and hope. The mood of a setting can heighten tension, amplify emotions, or provide contrast, shaping how events are perceived by readers.

In *The Road* by Cormac McCarthy, the post-apocalyptic setting of a burned, desolate world envelops every scene with a mood of despair and desolation. The ash-covered landscapes and the gray, lifeless skies not only frame the physical journey of the father and son but also amplify the emotional weight of their struggle for survival. The bleakness of the setting mirrors the themes of endurance and the fading flicker of hope in a world seemingly devoid of it, making the atmosphere a poignant backdrop to the characters' experiences.

Resources and Scarcity

The availability or lack of resources in a setting can drive events. A town facing a drought might see conflicts arise over water rights. Conversely, the discovery of a valuable resource, like gold, can trigger a rush of prospectors and the challenges that come with sudden wealth.

In Frank Herbert's *Dune*, the desert planet of Arrakis is the only source of the universe's most valuable resource, the spice melange. The scarcity of water and the abundance of spice drive the plot, influencing political power struggles, shaping the planet's culture, and impacting the characters' survival and strategies.

Encounters and Interactions

The setting determines who or what characters might encounter. A dense forest might hide mysterious creatures, while a bustling city offers encounters with a diverse array of individuals. These encounters can propel the plot, introducing new allies, adversaries, or elements of mystery. Did you put enough thought into your settings?

In *Dracula* by Bram Stoker, Jonathan Harker's journey to Transylvania and his stay at Dracula's castle introduce him to the supernatural horrors that permeate the story. The setting's isolation and the eerie encounters within the castle's walls set the stage for the unfolding events, as the novel's characters confront and combat the vampiric threat.

Catalysts for Change

Sometimes, the setting itself undergoes changes that influence events. A natural disaster, like an earthquake or flood, can dramatically alter the landscape and the trajectory of the story. Similarly, societal changes, like revolutions or reforms, can reshape the narrative landscape.

In *The Grapes of Wrath* by John Steinbeck, the Dust Bowl and the Great Depression are critical catalysts for change, driving the Joad family from their Oklahoma farm to seek a new life in California. The environmental and economic hardships of the era dictate the story's direction, highlighting how significant changes in setting can propel the narrative and its characters toward new destinies.

Setting is a powerful tool in the hands of a storyteller. It's not just a stage but a dynamic entity that interacts with characters and events. By understanding and harnessing the influence of setting, writers can craft narratives where the environment and plot are intricately intertwined, each shaping and being shaped by the other.

Chapter 6

The Role of History and Culture in Shaping Horror Stories

Imagine wandering through a landscape where the whispers of the past mingle with the shadows of the present, where each cobblestone and carved idol tells a tale not just of history but of the human psyche. This is the realm of horror that is deeply intertwined with the rich fabric of historical and cultural context. In this chapter, we embark on a journey to explore how the echoes of bygone eras and the customs of distant lands shape the eerie settings and complex characters that haunt the pages of horror fiction.

The Essence of Historical Times

Imagine setting your story in a time machine. Each era you visit offers a unique flavor to your horror concoction. Victorian England, with its foggy streets and rigid social norms, contrasts starkly with the vibrant and rebellious Roaring Twenties. These settings don't just dress the scene. They shape the very souls of your characters and the nightmares they face. Remember, horror fiction is a representation of the societal fears *of its time*.

Setting your horror story in a specific era isn't just about the backdrop—it's about immersing your characters and readers in a time where the world's understanding and reaction to the supernatural can be vastly different. Just think of the early superstitions regarding vampires rising from the graves. Take Victorian England, for instance, a popular setting for horror due to its mix of emerging scientific thought and deep-rooted superstitions. In Susan Hill's *The Woman in Black*, the fog-laden, marsh-surrounded Eel Marsh House is as much a character as Arthur Kipps, embodying the era's Gothic sensibilities and amplifying the story's haunting atmosphere.

Cultural Dos and Don'ts

Culture is like the unwritten rulebook of society, guiding what's considered normal and what's a big no-no. Picture a character from a conservative background caught in a love story in a place where holding hands is scandalous. The tension! The horror can stem from within, from the battle between desires and societal expectations.

Cultural norms and taboos can be a treasure trove for horror writers, creating internal and external conflicts for characters. In *Ring* by Koji Suzuki, the story taps into the Japanese cultural fear of curses and the supernatural, intertwined with modern anxieties about technology. The simple act of watching a videotape becomes a death sentence, reflecting a unique blend of traditional fears and contemporary life, showing how cultural norms can shape and escalate the horror in unexpected ways.

Who's Who in Society

Our characters don't live in a vacuum. They're part of a larger societal puzzle. Whether they're lords and ladies or rebels without a cause, their place in the world dictates their battles, alliances, and enemies. These societal roles can trap them or set them free, adding layers of intrigue to the horror narrative.

Societal roles and hierarchies can create a fertile ground for horror, as characters navigate the expectations and limitations of their station. Let's look at *Dracula* again, which showcases this brilliantly, with characters from various social sectors coming together to combat the vampire. The novel reflects the Victorian fascination with social order and the fear of its breakdown, using the Count's transgression of these boundaries (from invading homes to preying on the virtuous) to heighten the horror and suspense.

The Bigger Picture: Economics and Politics

Let's not forget the world stage—economic crises, political unrest, and wars shape lives in profound ways. A story set during the Great Depression, for instance, isn't just about the monsters lurking in the dark but also the real-world monsters of poverty and despair, adding depth and realism to the horror.

Economic downturns and political unrest can serve as a powerful backdrop for horror, adding layers of reality to the terror. *It* by Stephen King, where the socio-economic decay of Derry, Maine, mirrors the lurking evil of Pennywise, suggesting that the monster is as much a product of societal failure as it is a supernatural entity.

Trends, Arts, and Everyday Life

The zeitgeist of an era—its fashion, art, and day-to-day life—paints a vivid picture of the world our characters inhabit. From the elegance of the Renaissance to the gritty reality of the Industrial Revolution, these details add authenticity and texture to the setting, making the horror feel all the more real.

The everyday life, art, and fashion of an era can deeply influence a horror story's setting and mood. *The Picture of Dorian Gray* captures the hedonism of the late Victorian era, with the eponymous portrait reflecting the decay of societal and personal morals. The horror arises not just from the supernatural elements but from the stark portrayal of the era's obsession with beauty and youth, making the setting integral to the story's moral and physical terror.

Talking and Connecting

Communication is key, and in a horror story, the way characters talk and connect (or fail to) can be a source of tension. Imagine the misunderstandings and missed connections in a world without instant messaging, where every letter and telegram is a lifeline...or a harbinger of doom.

The way characters communicate in a horror story can significantly affect the plot and tension. In *Dracula*, Stoker uses letters, diaries, and telegrams to build suspense and convey the characters' isolation. This epistolary style reflects the communication limitations of the time, making each piece of correspondence crucial to the unfolding mystery and heightening the sense of dread as the characters struggle to piece together Dracula's plan.

Beliefs and Beyond

The spiritual and religious backdrop of a story can add a whole new dimension to character motivations and conflicts. Facing the supernatural, characters might question their beliefs, wrestle with moral dilemmas, and confront existential fears, adding depth to the horror.

Religious and spiritual beliefs can shape a horror story's conflict, character motivations, and themes. *The Exorcist* by William Peter Blatty explores the battle between modern skepticism and ancient faith through the harrowing ordeal of a young girl's possession. The novel delves into questions of faith, the power of evil, and the complexities of human nature, making the horror feel both profound and personal.

Celebrations and Traditions

Festivals and traditions provide a colorful canvas for horror stories. Imagine the contrast of a joyous celebration turned nightmarish, where cultural rituals become the setting for unspeakable horrors, enriching the narrative with a blend of beauty and terror.

Incorporating cultural festivals and traditions into a horror narrative can add a rich layer of symbolism and tension. *Something Wicked This Way Comes* by Ray Bradbury uses the allure and nostalgia of a traveling carnival to explore themes of desire, fear, and the loss of innocence. The story, set against the backdrop of an idyllic American Midwest town, becomes a nightmarish reflection on the dark side of wish fulfillment and the inherent horror in the corruption of childhood dreams.

As we peel back the layers of time, we find that each historical period offers its own unique brand of terror, influenced by the societal norms, technological advancements, and philosophical beliefs of the age. From the superstition-laden Middle Ages to the skepticism of the Enlightenment, each epoch provides a backdrop against which our deepest fears are projected and played out.

Culture, with its intricate tapestry of rituals, traditions, and taboos, adds another dimension to this landscape. It is within the boundaries of what is sacred and profane, whispered in folklore and enacted in festivals, that horror finds a fertile ground to bloom. The stories we tell around the fire, the monsters that lurk in our collective imaginations, are born from these cultural depths.

Together, history and culture are not just settings but characters in their own right, influencing the actions, motivations, and fates of those who dare to walk their haunted paths.

Chapter 7

Setting as Character

We've discussed this quite a few times already, but let's work on how to achieve this. In the world of storytelling, setting is often seen as just the backdrop against which the action unfolds.

The Essence of Setting as Character

To consider a setting as a character is to imbue it with qualities that go beyond mere geography and time. It must have a personality, desires, and even a will of its own. Like any character, it interacts with the protagonists and antagonists, shaping their decisions and growth. This dynamic environment not only enriches the narrative but also deepens the reader's engagement by making the world of the story feel alive and responsive.

Crafting a Living Setting:
- Just as characters have personalities, so should your setting. The oppressive heat of a desert planet can mirror the desperation of its inhabitants. A city's pulsing nightlife might reflect the chaotic energy of its denizens. By assigning mood and atmosphere, the setting becomes a mirror to the emotional landscape of your story.

- A setting with a character has a past, scars, and memories. The crumbling ruins of a once-great civilization speak of hubris and fall, influencing the narrative's themes and the characters' perceptions. An ancient forest might remember the passage of heroes and villains, its changing moods reflecting its long memory.

- While it may seem strange to attribute desires to a setting, doing so can add a layer of intrigue and depth. A haunted house might seem to yearn for peace, its restless spirits driving the plot toward resolution. A war-torn land could be seen as yearning for healing, influencing the characters' quests.

Examples from Literature and Film:
- Middle-earth in *The Lord of the Rings*: Tolkien's Middle-earth is a prime example of setting as character. Its vast landscapes, from the Shire's pastoral hills to Mordor's volcanic wastelands, are imbued with history and significance, directly impacting the characters' journeys and the story's themes of power, loss, and hope.

- The Overlook Hotel in *The Shining*: Stephen King's haunted hotel is a malevolent entity with desires and motives. Its eerie corridors and ghostly inhabitants exert a psychological influence on the Torrance family, driving the story's tension and horror.

- Pandora in *Avatar*: In James Cameron's film, the alien world of Pandora is a vibrant, living ecosystem. Its interconnected flora and fauna, reflective of the Na'vi's philosophy of balance and connection, play a crucial role in the narrative, opposing the human characters' exploitative goals.

Techniques for Developing a Living Setting

- Sensory Details: Engage all five senses to bring the setting to life. The scent of rain on dry earth, the cacophony of a bustling market, the chill of a shadowy forest—all contribute to the setting's personality and mood.

- Anthropomorphism: Assigning human traits to elements of your setting can make it more relatable and emotionally resonant. A city might 'wake up' as morning traffic fills its streets, or a mountain could 'watch over' an ancient town, suggesting protection and permanence.

- Interactive Environment: Show the setting reacting to the characters and vice versa. A storm might break out in a moment of emotional turmoil, or a secret garden might bloom anew as love grows between characters, illustrating the symbiotic relationship between them and their world.

Integrating Setting into the Narrative

For the setting to truly become a character, it must be integral to the plot and character development. Its features can provide obstacles or assistance, mirroring or contrasting the inner journeys of the characters. Its history can be a mystery to unravel, directly tied to the story's central conflict. Its mood can foreshadow events, setting the tone for the narrative's unfolding.

Challenges and Considerations

While a richly realized setting can immensely enhance a story, there are pitfalls to avoid. Beware of overwhelming the reader with excessive detail that stalls the narrative. Ensure that the setting serves the story, enhancing rather than overshadowing the characters and plot. Balance is key—let the setting breathe and influence the story without suffocating it.

When crafted with care and depth, the setting can transcend its traditional role to become a living entity that enriches the tapestry of the narrative. It becomes a mirror reflecting the themes, a stage influencing the drama, and a character that evolves with the story.

Chapter 8

Metaphors and Foreshadowing with Your Setting

The Art of Metaphor

In the realm of creative writing, the metaphor stands as one of the most potent tools in a writer's arsenal. It is the bridge that connects the mundane to the magnificent, transforming the simple into the sublime. Metaphors allow writers to infuse their prose with layers of meaning and emotion, to elevate their descriptions beyond the confines of literal language. Teaching the art of metaphor is not just about encouraging writers to draw comparisons, however. It's about nurturing a way of seeing and thinking that reveals the interconnectedness of all things.

The Power of Metaphor

Metaphors have the power to illuminate the unseen and articulate the inexpressible. They serve as a conduit for the imagination, enabling writers to convey complex ideas and emotions in a manner that is both accessible and profound. A well-crafted metaphor can turn a phrase into a painting, and a sentence into a symphony. It is the alchemy that turns leaden words into literary gold.

Seeing the World Anew

To harness the power of metaphor, writers must learn to see the world anew. They must look beyond the surface of things, to find the hidden threads that bind the world together. A leaf might not just be a leaf, but a green ship sailing on the winds of autumn. The night sky is not merely a void dotted with stars, but a velvet canvas sprinkled with celestial fireflies. By reimagining the ordinary, writers can give readers a glimpse of the extraordinary.

Finding the Universal in the Specific

Metaphors are most effective when they resonate with the reader on a universal level. The key is to find those connections between disparate things that touch upon a shared human experience. A writer might describe the end of a love affair as the final act of a play, the curtain falling on a stage now empty of actors. This not only paints a vivid picture but also taps into the universal themes of loss and finality.

The Challenge of Originality

Facing the challenge of originality head-on, especially when it comes to metaphors, is like trying to find a new path through a well-trodden forest. Literature is brimming with metaphors that, while once vibrant and thought-provoking, have now become all too familiar, losing their sparkle along the way. The trick to breaking free from the grip of cliché is for writers to dig deep into the treasure trove of their own life stories, emotions, and unique ways of seeing the world. It's about making the metaphor your own, painting it with the colors of your individual perspective. This not only breathes new life into the metaphor but also gives readers a fresh pair of glasses through which to view the world.

It's a journey of exploration, one where writers are tasked with uncovering and sharing their distinctive voices and experiences, turning the familiar on its head and illuminating it with a new light.

Metaphor as the Soul of Language

At its heart, metaphor is the soul of language. It is what gives prose its poetic quality and what makes descriptions sing. When a writer describes a character's hope as "a flickering candle in the vast darkness of despair," they do more than paint a picture—they evoke an emotional landscape. Metaphor invites readers to experience the world through the writer's eyes, to feel the texture of their thoughts and the color of their emotions.

Teaching the art of metaphor is, in many ways, teaching the art of seeing. It's about opening writers' eyes to the beauty and poetry that lie hidden in the everyday. It's about encouraging them to weave connections that reveal deeper truths and to express those truths in language that moves, surprises, and delights. In the end, the ability to craft beautiful metaphors is not just a skill. It's a way of engaging with the world, a testament to the writer's imagination and insight. It is, perhaps, what makes the written word so enduringly powerful.

Foreshadowing Through Environment

Imagine walking through a dense forest, and suddenly, the path ahead is shrouded in an unusually thick fog. Or picture a character entering a grand mansion, but one room, despite its opulence, is oddly cold. These aren't just random details. They're the environment subtly hinting at what's to come. Using setting as a tool for foreshadowing is a crafty technique that writers employ to give readers a taste of the future, without revealing the whole dish.

- Nature's Whispers: The natural world is a treasure trove of foreshadowing tools. A sudden change in weather, like an unexpected storm brewing on what was a clear day, can hint at turmoil or conflict on the horizon. Birds suddenly taking flight can signal an impending disturbance. Even the phases of the moon, with its cycle of growth and decline, can be symbolic of the ebbs and flows in a character's journey.

- Architectural Omens: Buildings and structures, too, can be prophetic. A broken step in an otherwise pristine staircase might hint at an overlooked flaw or danger. A locked room in a house could suggest buried secrets or upcoming revelations. Even the layout of a town or city, with its twists, turns, and dead ends, can mirror the complexities and challenges a character might soon face.

- Colors and Atmosphere: The palette of the setting can be incredibly telling. A room painted in vibrant red might exude passion, danger, or significant change, while a landscape dominated by cool blues and grays might hint at introspection, sadness, or a challenge that requires calm and strategy. The general vibe of a place, whether it's an eerie silence in a usually bustling market or an unexplained chill in a warm setting, can set the stage for upcoming events.

- Cultural and Historical Hints: Sometimes, the history of a place or its cultural significance can be a foreshadowing tool. An old battlefield, though now serene, might hint at upcoming conflicts. A festival or ritual, with its specific customs, can foreshadow events or outcomes related to its significance.

Incorporating these hints through setting requires a delicate touch. It's like leaving breadcrumbs for the readers, not a full trail. Too obvious, and the suspense is lost; too subtle, and the hint might go unnoticed. But when done right, using the environment as foreshadowing enriches the narrative, creating a layered reading experience. It's a gentle nudge to the reader's intuition, making them feel connected to the story's pulse, anticipating what's to come, and reveling in the satisfaction when their inklings come to fruition.

Chapter 9
Symbolism in Setting

In the realm of literature, settings transcend their role as mere backdrops, evolving into complex symbols that resonate with broader themes and mirror the emotional landscapes of characters. This use of setting infuses narratives with a rich layer of meaning, offering readers a tapestry of symbols through which deeper insights and emotions can be gleaned. The artful integration of symbolism within setting enables authors to communicate intricate ideas and feelings implicitly, inviting readers to engage in an interpretative dance that unveils the narrative's multifaceted depth. Want to know how to raise your craft to the next level? Symbolism is a big step forward.

Nature and Landscapes

Nature, in its myriad forms, serves as a potent symbol, reflecting the human condition and thematic undercurrents. A desolate desert landscape might echo the profound isolation or despondency of a character, while the vibrant life of a blossoming garden could signify personal growth or a period of rejuvenation. The tumultuousness of stormy seas often mirrors the stormy internal struggles of a character, juxtaposed against the serene tranquility of a still lake, which may symbolize a moment of reflection or inner peace.

Buildings and Architecture

The symbolism of man-made structures is equally compelling, with each edifice telling its own story. A dilapidated mansion may stand as a testament to the decline of a once-prominent lineage or the fleeting nature of material wealth, whereas the imposing stature of a skyscraper could be emblematic of human ambition, the relentless pursuit of progress, or a critique of societal vanity.

Seasons and Time of Day

The passage of time, marked by the cyclical change of seasons or the diurnal shift from dawn to dusk, often parallels the narrative arc or the evolution of characters. The hopeful light of dawn may herald new beginnings or the promise of redemption, while the encroaching shadows of dusk could signal impending endings or the onset of peril. The barren chill of winter frequently signifies a period of dormancy or loss, contrasted with the rejuvenative promise of spring, which brings with it themes of renewal and rebirth.

Objects within Settings

Within these symbolic landscapes, individual objects can emerge as beacons of meaning. A solitary tree in an expansive field may symbolize the enduring strength and solitude of a character, while an unyielding locked door might represent unfulfilled potential or the secrets that lie buried beneath the surface.

Colors and Atmosphere

The palette of a setting, with its deliberate use of color, can evoke specific emotional responses or symbolize underlying themes. A setting awash in hues of red might evoke the intensity of passion, the imminent threat of danger, or the simmering undercurrent of rage, while a landscape painted in shades of blue could convey a sense of serenity or deep-seated melancholy. The ambiguity of a fog-enshrouded setting might reflect the prevailing sense of confusion or the elusive nature of truth.

Cultural and Historical Significance

Settings steeped in historical or cultural significance carry the weight of collective memory and societal values. The haunting silence of a battlefield may serve as a somber reminder of the atrocities of war and the sacrifices made, while the sacred quiet of a temple might embody the enduring presence of faith and tradition within a community.

Juxtaposition of Settings

The deliberate contrast between settings can serve as a powerful narrative device, symbolizing internal conflicts or thematic dichotomies. A character navigating the frenetic pace of urban life while yearning for the pastoral tranquility of rural environs may embody the universal struggle between the lure of ambition and the call to simplicity.

When settings are imbued with symbolic value, they elevate the story, crafting a literary experience that is both immersive and resonant, leaving a lasting imprint on the reader's imagination.

Chapter 10
Transitions in Setting

In the art of storytelling, transitions between settings are much more than mere logistical shifts. They are the narrative threads that weave together the fabric of our tale. These transitions act as bridges that guide readers from one scene to the next, and carry with them the potential to enrich the story with depth, nuance, and rhythm. Far from being simple changes in location, transitions are pivotal moments that can signal shifts in the narrative's direction, illuminate character development, or introduce new layers of complexity.

Why Transitions Matter

Transitions in setting are akin to scene changes in a film, marking a shift in the narrative's focus and pacing. They serve as indicators of change, heralding new challenges, environments, and opportunities for character interaction. A well-crafted transition can heighten the reader's anticipation, signaling that something significant is on the horizon, whether it's an impending confrontation, a pivotal revelation, or a shift in the protagonist's journey.

Tips for Crafting Smooth Transitions
- Narrative Bridges: Seamlessly connecting two settings involves more than physical movement. It's about creating a narrative continuum. Employing a shared emotion, a recurring motif, or a piece of dialogue

that resonates across scenes can provide a smooth passage, linking the old and new settings with subtlety and coherence.

- Pacing: The tempo of your transition can dramatically influence the narrative's tension and flow. A swift, abrupt shift might inject a sense of urgency and suspense, while a more measured transition can offer the reader a reflective pause, a moment to breathe and take stock of the unfolding story.

- Character Perspective: The transition is a mirror reflecting the character's inner world. Their perceptions, emotions, and reactions to the change in setting can deepen the reader's understanding of their character arc, offering insights into their fears, hopes, and motivations.

- Foreshadowing: A hint or a whisper of what's to come can be a powerful tool in setting the stage for the next scene. This preparatory touch not only builds anticipation but also ensures that the reader is mentally and emotionally aligned with the narrative's trajectory.

- Flashbacks and Flashforwards: These narrative techniques can serve dual purposes, acting both as bridges and as layers of storytelling. By temporarily transporting the reader to a different time, they provide context and depth, enriching the primary narrative thread upon return.

- Thematic Links: Weaving common themes or motifs through different settings can stitch the narrative together, maintaining a sense of continuity and cohesion. Even in the midst of diverse locales, these thematic echoes can resonate with the reader, reinforcing the story's underlying message.

A notable example of an effective transition in modern horror fiction can be found in Stephen King's novel *The Shining*. King masterfully uses transitions to amplify the horror and build tension throughout the story. One particular transition that stands out is when Jack Torrance, the protagonist, moves through the different settings within the Overlook Hotel. King transitions from the opulence of the hotel's main areas, filled with reminders of its grand past, into the more sinister, secluded parts of the hotel, like the hedge maze and Room 217.

These transitions are not merely physical movements from one location to another but are charged with psychological implications, reflecting Jack's descent into madness. For instance, when Jack first enters the infamous Room 217, King doesn't just move the character into a new setting; he shifts the atmosphere from the mundane to the menacing. The description of the room's eerie stillness and the sense of something waiting sets a chilling tone. This transition is made more powerful by the stark contrast with the previous scene's relative normalcy, thus deepening the horror and drawing the reader further into the unsettling world of the Overlook Hotel.

Through these carefully crafted transitions, King not only moves the story forward but also layers the narrative with a growing sense of dread, making the setting itself a character that mirrors the protagonist's psychological unraveling.

The Impact of Transitions

- Character Development: As characters navigate new environments, their responses can unveil facets of their personality, beliefs, and growth, offering a multi-dimensional view of their journey.

- Plot Progression: Strategic transitions can propel the plot forward, introducing fresh dynamics, conflicts, or resolutions that keep the narrative momentum alive.

- Tone and Atmosphere: The atmosphere of a new setting, and the transition into it, can subtly alter the story's mood, coloring the narrative with different emotional hues and textures.

- Symbolism: Settings often bear symbolic weight, and the transition between them can highlight these deeper meanings, enriching the narrative with layers of symbolic significance.

Transitions are not mere narrative necessities, though. they are opportunities to enrich and enliven the story. By thoughtfully crafting these shifts, writers can enhance the narrative's cohesion, depth, and resonance. As we guide our readers through the evolving landscapes of our stories, let us remember that each transition is a chance to reinvigorate the narrative, to surprise and delight, and to weave a richer, more compelling tapestry. May your transitions be as fluid and meaningful as the stories they serve.

Chapter 11

Mirroring Narrative and Character Growth through Evolving Settings

The transformation of settings in a narrative is a powerful storytelling device, akin to the growth and evolution we witness in characters. Just as individuals undergo changes, maturing and adapting over time, the environments within a story can evolve, reflecting broader narrative shifts and the developmental arcs of its characters. This dynamic interplay between setting and story enriches the narrative, adding layers of depth and meaning that resonate with the theme of change and progression.

Nature's Dance

Nature's inherent cycle of growth and decay serves as a poignant metaphor for change. The journey of a sapling to a towering tree within the span of a narrative can symbolize resilience, growth, or the inexorable passage of time. Similarly, the transition of seasons from the rejuvenating bloom of spring to the desolate quiet of winter can mirror a character's journey from naivety to the sobering embrace of reality. These natural evolutions are subtle yet powerful, reflecting the organic changes characters undergo.

Architectural Progress (or Decay)

The evolution of architectural landscapes within a story can offer a mirror to the internal and external changes of its characters. The expansion of a quaint town into a bustling metropolis may symbolize ambition, progress, or the darker sides of modernization, such as greed or environmental neglect. In contrast, the decay of once-grand edifices can reflect themes of loss, the ravages of time, or societal decline. These transformations in setting can serve as a backdrop that parallels or contrasts the fortunes and choices of the characters, adding a rich backdrop to the narrative tapestry.

Cultural and Societal Shifts

As characters navigate their journeys, the cultural and societal fabric of their world might shift alongside them. A narrative that captures the liberalization of a conservative society can reflect broader themes of progress, enlightenment, and the breaking of old chains. Conversely, a setting that becomes more oppressive or constrained over time can signal looming threats, societal regression, or the loss of freedom, serving as a commentary on the characters' struggles against these tides.

Personal Spaces Tell Personal Tales

The personal environments of characters, such as their homes or workspaces, are direct extensions of their inner selves. A meticulously kept room descending into disarray can subtly signify a character's psychological unraveling or overwhelming challenges. Conversely, the transformation of a chaotic space into one of order and peace can symbolize a character's journey toward resolution, clarity, or personal growth, making the setting an intimate stage for character development.

Landmarks and Legacy: The Resonance of Place

Sometimes, the most profound changes in setting are not physical but symbolic. Locations marked by past events can evolve in their significance to the characters and the community. A site of tragedy may become a beacon of hope, remembrance, or new beginnings, its physical sameness belied by the depth of its emotional and symbolic transformation.

In weaving the evolution of settings into the narrative fabric, writers paint on a canvas that shifts and grows with the story. This dynamic landscape requires a keen awareness of the narrative's past, present, and potential futures. When artfully integrated, these evolving settings become silent narrators, enriching the story with their silent testimony to the inevitable flux of life and the enduring spirit of growth and change. They remind readers that in the world of the story, as in life, nothing remains static—everything is subject to the beautiful, relentless march of change. This of course works really well in a series.

Chapter 12

Small Spaces vs. Expansive Realms

Every tale we spin is set upon a stage, and the choice of that stage—be it a tight, intimate corner or a sprawling, boundless realm—can shape the narrative's heartbeat. As storytellers, we must decide whether to draw our readers into the close, whispered secrets of a confined space or to let them soar over vast, open landscapes. Both have their magic, and both come with their own set of tools and challenges.

Small Spaces

These are the nooks and crannies of our stories. Imagine a dimly lit study, a narrow alleyway echoing with footsteps, a crowded attic filled with memories, or the inside of a rain-splattered car.

Strengths:

- Such spaces can turn up the emotional heat, creating a cauldron of heightened feelings and interactions.

- With a limited canvas, every brushstroke counts. Writers can paint with rich, evocative details, making the setting pulse with life.

- Characters, being elbow-to-elbow, can't easily escape each other, leading to raw, unfiltered exchanges.

Challenges:
- There's only so much room to maneuver, which can hem in characters and action.

- It's a dance to keep the narrative fresh and avoid feeling like a stuck record.

Expansive Realms

Here, the world stretches out, limitless. We're talking about bustling cities humming with life, open meadows kissed by the sun, or even galaxies twinkling in the vastness of space.

Strengths:
- Such settings are a smorgasbord of locations, cultures, and challenges, offering a rich tapestry for our tales.

- Big settings can house big stories—heroic quests, intricate dramas, and sprawling adventures.

- Characters can roam, discovering new terrains, challenges, and allies on their path.

Challenges:
- With so much on offer, there's a risk of scattering the narrative's focus or burying the reader in minutiae.

- Crafting a vast world means ensuring its history, culture, and geography all sing from the same song sheet.

Striking the Right Note

Whether you're crafting a tale set in the hushed confines of a secret chamber or one that gallops across continents, the trick lies in knowing which setting serves the story's heart best. Some narratives demand the intimacy of whispered confessions in shadowed corners, while others need the grand sweep of epic landscapes.

From the tiniest of spaces to the grandest of realms, our choice of setting isn't just a backdrop—it's a character in its own right. It shapes our story, molds our characters, and sets the tone. By mastering the dance between the intimate and the expansive, we can craft tales that resonate deeply, pulling readers into the very soul of our narrative.

Cityscapes and Countrysides

Picture this: the hustle and bustle of a city, with its towering skyscrapers, neon lights, and the constant hum of traffic. Now, juxtapose that with the serene beauty of a countryside, where rolling hills, chirping birds, and the gentle rustle of leaves paint a picture of tranquility. The contrast between man-made urban environments and natural landscapes isn't just visual; it's deeply symbolic and can be a goldmine for storytelling.

Cities, with their concrete jungles and fast-paced life, often symbolize progress, ambition, and the human desire to reach for the stars. They're places of opportunity, where dreams can be chased, and fortunes made. But they also come with their own set of challenges. The noise, the crowds, and the relentless pace can sometimes feel suffocating. It's no wonder that stories set in cities often explore themes of isolation amidst the crowd, the struggle to find one's identity, or the moral dilemmas posed by modern life.

On the flip side, natural settings, like quaint villages, dense forests, or serene beaches, often evoke a sense of peace and simplicity. They remind us of a time when life was less complicated, and our connection to nature was more profound. But don't be fooled by the calm exterior; nature has its own set of rules. In the wild, it's often about survival, the circle of life, and the respect nature commands. Stories set in these landscapes can delve into man's primal instincts, the beauty and brutality of the natural world, or the age-old conflict between civilization and wilderness.

When these two worlds collide, that's where the magic happens. Think of a city dweller who finds themselves in a remote village, grappling with the slower pace and the customs of the locals. Or a country person stepping into the city for the first time, wide-eyed at the marvels of modernity but also overwhelmed by its complexities. These fish-out-of-water scenarios are ripe for exploration, humor, and even conflict.

Moreover, the ongoing tug-of-war between urban expansion and nature's preservation is a theme that resonates deeply in today's world. As cities expand, forests shrink, and the balance between man-made and natural gets skewed. This can lead to stories that explore environmental issues, the consequences of unchecked urbanization, or even the simple longing for a return to nature.

In a nutshell, whether it's the glittering lights of a metropolis or the untouched beauty of a mountain valley, settings play a crucial role in shaping the narrative. By understanding the contrasts and conflicts between man-made and natural environments, writers can craft stories that are not only engaging but also reflective of the world we live in. After all, isn't storytelling all about capturing the essence of the human experience, whether amidst skyscrapers or under the canopy of stars?

Chapter 13

When the Environment Becomes the Challenge

Ever been caught in a sudden downpour without an umbrella? Or tried to navigate your way through a thick fog? Nature, with all its unpredictability, often throws challenges our way, and it's no different in the world of story-telling. From the vast emptiness of deserts to the icy grip of harsh winters, environmental challenges can add depth, tension, and excitement to our tales.

Imagine a serene scene, where two characters are having a heart-to-heart. Suddenly, the skies darken, and a torrential downpour interrupts their crucial conversation. It's not just about the rain. It's about the sudden shift in mood, the urgency, and the drama that comes with it. Storms, in particular, have a way of heightening emotions and accelerating events. A coastal town preparing for an approaching hurricane can become a backdrop for panic, solidarity, and resilience.

But it's not just storms that can stir the pot. Think of the vast, seemingly endless expanse of a desert. At first glance, it might seem monotonous—just sand and sun. But the desert is a place of extremes. The scorching heat of the day gives way to freezing nights. Water, which we often take for granted, becomes a precious commodity. And the mirages? They can play tricks on the mind, making characters question their reality. The desert, with its challenges, can become a crucible, testing the determination and resourcefulness of those who dare to cross it.

Then there's winter, which isn't always about cozy fireplaces and hot cocoa. The beauty of snow-covered landscapes can be deceptive. Harsh winters bring their own set of challenges – from blizzards that can disorient even the most seasoned traveler to frozen lakes that pose a danger with every step. A journey through a snow-laden forest can become a battle against nature, where every gust of cold wind and every snowdrift can push characters to their limits.

Of course, the world is full of other natural challenges. Dense forests where every turn looks the same, treacherous mountain paths that test the stamina, or even the looming threat of a volcanic eruption. Each of these environmental obstacles can be used to heighten conflict, challenge characters, and drive the narrative forward.

In essence, nature offers writers a treasure trove of scenarios to spice up their stories. It's not just about adding an external challenge—it's about how characters react, adapt, and overcome these hurdles. By weaving in these environmental curveballs, stories can resonate more deeply, reflecting the age-old human struggle against the mighty forces of nature. So, the next time you're crafting a tale, consider letting Mother Nature play a starring role. She's got a lot of tricks up her sleeve!

Section 3
Point of View

The essence of horror fiction lies not just in the tales of the macabre and the supernatural but in the way these tales are told. At the heart of this narrative alchemy is the point of view (POV), the lens through which the story is unveiled to the reader. It is the POV that invites the reader into the story, guiding them through a carefully constructed landscape of fear, suspense, and sometimes, the outright grotesque. The choice of POV can transform a straightforward tale into a multi-layered narrative, enriching the story with depth, emotion, and a palpable sense of dread.

In the realm of horror, the POV does more than narrate. It shapes the reader's experience, dictating how much they know, how closely they identify with characters, and how they interpret the unfolding events. It is a powerful tool in the horror writer's arsenal, capable of amplifying suspense, deepening character development, and enhancing the thematic impact of the story.

The main POVs employed in storytelling are first-person, second-person, third-person limited, and third-person omniscient, each offering unique advantages and challenges in horror fiction:

- First-Person POV offers an intimate glimpse into the narrator's mind, making their fears and discoveries our own. This POV can create a claustrophobic atmosphere and a sense of immediacy, drawing readers directly into the heart of the terror. The first-person narrative is particularly effective in psychological horror, where the reliability of the narrator can be a central theme, adding layers of complexity and uncertainty.

• Second-Person POV, the rarest in fiction, directly addresses the reader as 'you', placing them in the story. This unusual perspective can be disorienting and immersive, making the reader an active participant in the horror narrative. It challenges the traditional boundaries between the story and the reader, potentially heightening the emotional impact and making the horror more personal.

• Third-Person Limited POV allows the writer to focus on the experiences and perceptions of a single character at a time, offering a balance between the intimacy of the first-person POV and the broader perspective of the third-person omniscient. This POV can heighten suspense by limiting the reader's knowledge to that of the focal character, making every revelation and hidden danger more impactful.

• Third-Person Omniscient POV provides a 'god-like' perspective, offering insights into the thoughts, feelings, and motivations of multiple characters. While this can reduce the immediacy of the horror, it allows for a more complex and layered narrative, weaving together multiple storylines and perspectives to create a rich, textured tapestry of fear.

Each POV carries its own set of strengths and can be leveraged to enhance different aspects of a horror story. The choice of POV is a strategic decision that can shape the reader's journey, influence the pacing and tension of the narrative, and ultimately, determine how the horror unfolds. In the following sections, we will delve deeper into each POV, exploring their unique contributions to horror fiction and guiding you on how to harness their potential to craft stories that linger in the imagination long after the final page is turned.

Chapter 1

Understanding Point of View

The narrative perspective, or point of view (POV), is the vantage point from which a story is told. It is the "eye" through which we, as readers, see the narrative world. This choice is fundamental in storytelling, as it shapes every aspect of the narrative, from the plot and character development to the reader's emotional engagement. In horror fiction, where the aim is to evoke fear, suspense, and a sense of the uncanny, the POV becomes even more crucial. It can determine how close we get to the horror itself, how we interpret the characters' actions and motivations, and how we experience the unfolding of the narrative's darker elements.

Definitions and Characteristics of Different POVs

First-Person POV is characterized by the use of "I" or "we." In this POV, the narrator is a character within the story, offering a personal account of the events. This perspective can range from a protagonist directly involved in the action to a peripheral observer offering a more detached recounting. The first-person POV provides a deep dive into the narrator's psyche, presenting their perceptions, thoughts, and emotions from the inside out. This intimate access can make the horrors experienced by the narrator more visceral and immediate for the reader.

Second-Person POV uses the pronoun "you," turning the reader into the protagonist. This POV is less common in literature due to its direct address, which can feel jarring or intrusive. However, when used effectively, especially in horror, it can create a uniquely immersive experience. The reader is no longer a mere observer but an active participant in the narrative, making the fear and suspense more personal and direct.

Third-Person Limited POV employs "he," "she," or "they" and is limited to the perspective of one character at a time. The narrative may shift between characters from one section or chapter to another, but within a given section, it remains bound to a single character's perspective. This POV combines the external perspective of third-person narration with the intimacy of first-person, allowing the reader to get close to the character's experiences and emotions without being confined to their knowledge and biases.

Third-Person Omniscient POV also uses "he," "she," or "they" but offers a godlike perspective, with the narrator having access to the thoughts, feelings, and motivations of any or all characters. This POV can provide a comprehensive view of the narrative world and its inhabitants, presenting a multifaceted perspective on the story's events. While it can dilute the immediacy of the horror experience, it allows for a rich, layered storytelling that can enhance the thematic depth and complexity of the narrative.

The Role of POV in Shaping the Reader's Experience

The choice of POV in horror fiction is instrumental in determining the reader's journey through the story. Each POV shapes the reader's connection with the characters, the level of information available to the reader, and the intensity and proximity of the horror experience.

First-Person POV creates a strong empathetic link between the reader and the narrator. The reader sees the world through the narrator's eyes, feels their fear, and shares in their discoveries and dread. This POV can make the horror more immediate and personal, as readers are confined to the narrator's perspective, sharing in their limited knowledge and uncertainties. The use of an unreliable narrator can further enhance the suspense, leaving the reader questioning what is real and what is a product of the narrator's perception.

Second-Person POV places the reader in the heart of the narrative, transforming the reading experience into a personal ordeal. This POV can make the horror more confrontational, as the readers are compelled to imagine themselves in the terrifying situations depicted in the story. The direct address can break down the barriers between the narrative and the reader, making the horror feel more immediate and invasive.

Third-Person Limited POV offers a balance between the intimacy of first-person and the broader perspective of third-person omniscient. By focusing closely on one character's experiences at a time, this POV allows readers to engage deeply with the characters' emotional states while maintaining the ability to shift focus and gain new perspectives. This can be particularly effective in horror, where shifting the focal character can reveal new facets of the horror or heighten suspense as readers anticipate horrors that the focal character has yet to discover.

Third-Person Omniscient POV provides a panoramic view of the narrative world, allowing readers to understand the horror from multiple angles. This POV can dilute the immediacy of the horror experience by distancing the reader from the characters' direct experiences. However, it also allows for a more complex and nuanced exploration of the horror, showing how it affects different characters and weaving together multiple storylines to create a rich tapestry of fear.

In horror fiction, the POV not only shapes the narrative structure but also plays a pivotal role in creating atmosphere and tension. It influences how readers perceive and react to the story's events, characters, and underlying themes. By carefully choosing and implementing the POV, horror writers can control the pacing of their narrative, the revelation of information, and the intensity of the horror experience, crafting stories that captivate and terrify in equal measure.

The choice of POV is a strategic one, with each offering its own set of tools for horror storytelling. Whether it's the immersive intimacy of first-person, the disorienting directness of second-person, the focused engagement of third-person limited, or the expansive scope of third-person omniscient, the POV sets the stage for the horror to unfold. It is through this narrative lens that the dark heart of the story is revealed, and the reader's journey through the shadowy corridors of fear is shaped.

Chapter 2

The Strengths of Each POV in Horror

In the craft of horror writing, the choice of point of view (POV) is not merely a technical decision. It's a gateway to the soul of the story. Each POV carries with it a unique set of capabilities, shaping the narrative's atmosphere, the reader's connection to the characters, and the intensity of the horror experience. This chapter delves into the strengths of first-person, second-person, third-person limited, and third-person omniscient POVs in horror fiction, illustrating how each can be wielded to amplify the terror and depth of the narrative.

First-Person POV: Intimacy and Immediacy

The first-person POV offers a window directly into the protagonist's mind, forging an intimate bond between character and reader. This closeness allows the horror to unfold within the confines of the protagonist's personal experience, making every shadow deeper and every whisper louder. The immediacy of this POV can transform abstract fears into palpable terror, as readers are not mere observers but participants in the protagonist's ordeal.

This perspective is particularly potent in psychological horror, where the line between reality and delusion often blurs. Through the lens of an unreliable narrator, the narrative can twist and turn, ensnaring the reader in a web of doubt and paranoia. Stories like Edgar Allan Poe's "The Tell-Tale Heart" exemplify how the first-person POV can be used to immerse readers in the narrator's fractured psyche, making the horror as much about the struggle within as the external threats. Unless you have chapters written in the point of view of other characters, the reader can not know anything that the focal character doesn't know.

Second-Person POV: Immersiveness and Complicity

The second-person POV, with its use of "you," creates a compelling narrative perspective that can immerse readers in the horror story. This rare but impactful POV can dissolve the boundary between the reader and the text, pulling the reader into the fabric of the narrative. In horror, this immersion can make the experiences more visceral, as readers are compelled to inhabit the roles laid out for them, making each decision, feeling each fear, as if it were their own.

This POV can also engender a sense of complicity, implicating the reader in the narrative's dark unfoldings. It's a daring approach that, when executed skillfully, can leave a lasting impression, transforming the act of reading into an act of living through the horror story. This POV works well for short stories or flash fiction, but tends to be too much for most readers in longer length pieces.

Third-Person Limited POV: Flexibility and Focus

The third-person limited POV offers a versatile narrative tool, combining the external perspective of third-person narration with the internal depth of first-person. By focusing on the experiences and perceptions of one character at a time, this POV can delve deeply into the emotional and psychological landscape of the protagonist while retaining the ability to shift focus, offering fresh perspectives and insights.

In horror fiction, this POV can maintain suspense and tension by limiting the reader's knowledge to that of the focal character. This constrained viewpoint can magnify the horror elements, as readers, bound to the protagonist's side, face each unknown and terror as it unfolds. Remember, if the focal character can't see what's happening behind him/her, then neither can the reader.

Third-Person Omniscient POV: The God's Eye View

The third-person omniscient POV, with its all-seeing, all-knowing perspective, offers a panoramic view of the narrative world. This godlike viewpoint can weave together the thoughts, feelings, and experiences of multiple characters, creating a rich, multi-layered tapestry of horror. The omniscient POV can reveal the full scope of the terror that awaits, instilling a sense of dread and inevitability as the narrative threads converge toward a chilling nexus.

This perspective is particularly suited to complex horror narratives, where the interplay of different characters and storylines can build a more intricate and immersive world. The broad view provided by the third-person omniscient POV can also highlight the thematic underpinnings of the horror, drawing connections and contrasts between characters and events that enrich the narrative's depth and resonance.

Each POV brings its unique strengths to the horror genre, offering different pathways to explore fear, suspense, and the unknown. The first-person POV, with its intimate immediacy, can make the horror personal and visceral. The second-person POV, though less common, can immerse and implicate the reader in the narrative in unparalleled ways. The third-person limited POV offers a balanced approach, allowing for deep character exploration while maintaining narrative flexibility. Lastly, the third-person omniscient POV provides a comprehensive view of the horror landscape, weaving complex stories with multiple characters and layers.

The choice of POV is a fundamental decision in horror writing, one that can shape the narrative's impact and effectiveness. By understanding the strengths and potential of each POV, writers can craft horror stories that resonate deeply with readers, leveraging the power of perspective to heighten the terror and deepen the narrative's emotional impact. As we explore further in the following chapters, the alignment of POV with story type, the exploration of canonical examples, and the understanding of common pitfalls and best practices will further illuminate the critical role of POV in crafting compelling horror fiction.

Chapter 3

Matching POV to Story Type

In horror fiction, the alignment of point of view (POV) with the story's sub-genre and thematic elements is pivotal. The chosen perspective not only shapes the narrative's voice but also deeply influences the reader's engagement, the pacing of the plot, and the intensity of the horror experience. This chapter explores how different POVs resonate with specific horror sub-genres, impacting the story's delivery and the reader's immersion.

Psychological Horror

Psychological horror, which delves into the complexities of the human mind, often finds a natural ally in the first-person POV. This perspective allows for a deep exploration of the protagonist's psyche, making their fears, delusions, and unraveling mental state intimately accessible to the reader. The inherent immediacy of first-person narration amplifies the suspense and confusion, as readers are confined to the narrator's potentially unreliable perspective. This limitation can be a powerful tool, creating a claustrophobic atmosphere where reality is constantly in question, enhancing the psychological horror's impact.

Interactive or Experimental Horror

The second-person POV, though rare in traditional narratives, offers unique opportunities in interactive or experimental horror. By directly addressing the reader as "you," this POV creates a compelling sense of participation, making the horror experience personal and immediate. In stories where the reader's choices influence the outcome, or in narratives that aim to break the fourth wall, the second-person perspective can heighten the sense of dread and complicity. This POV can transform the narrative into a hauntingly immersive experience, where the boundary between the reader and the story blurs.

Gothic and Supernatural Horror

Gothic and supernatural horror, with their emphasis on atmosphere, setting, and suspense, often benefit from the third-person limited POV. This perspective allows writers to craft a detailed and atmospheric depiction of the eerie settings typical of gothic horror while maintaining a close connection to the characters' inner fears and experiences. The third-person limited POV offers the flexibility to shift focus between characters, providing varied insights into the supernatural elements without revealing too much too soon, thereby maintaining suspense and enhancing the mysterious, otherworldly atmosphere.

Epic or Cosmic Horror

Epic horror stories, including cosmic horror, which deals with incomprehensible, universe-spanning terrors, are well-suited to the third-person omniscient POV. This perspective allows for a broad, god-like view of the narrative, encompassing multiple storylines, characters, and, often, vast cosmic scales. The omniscient POV can convey the sheer enormity and inevitability of the horror facing the characters, providing a sense of despair and insignificance that is central to cosmic horror. By weaving together various characters' experiences and reactions to the unfolding terror, the narrative can achieve a layered, complex portrayal of the horror that transcends individual perspectives.

Impact on Pacing, Tension, and Engagement

The choice of POV not only matches the thematic and atmospheric needs of the horror sub-genre but also significantly impacts the story's pacing and tension. A first-person narrative might offer a rapid, visceral pacing, keeping readers closely tied to the protagonist's moment-to-moment experiences. In contrast, the second-person POV can create an unconventional pacing, drawing readers into an active role within the story. Third-person limited allows for a more controlled pacing, focusing on key characters' experiences while withholding information to build suspense. The omniscient perspective might provide a slower, more deliberate pacing, offering a comprehensive view that gradually reveals the horror's magnitude.

Each POV invites a different level of engagement from the reader, from the intimate complicity of first-person to the broad, detached overview provided by third-person omniscient. By carefully matching the POV to the horror story type, writers can craft narratives that not only resonate with the chosen sub-genre's conventions but also maximize the emotional and psychological impact on the reader. The following chapters will delve into practical examples, common pitfalls, and strategies for selecting the most effective POV for your horror story, further exploring how this crucial narrative choice shapes the dark tapestry of horror fiction.

In the exploration of point of view (POV) within horror fiction, examining seminal works provides invaluable insights into how narrative perspective shapes the horror experience. This chapter delves into classic horror literature, highlighting the effective use of various POVs to enhance thematic depth, character development, and emotional impact. Through these examples, we can observe the nuanced ways in which POV influences the reader's engagement and the story's atmosphere.

First-Person POV: "The Tell-Tale Heart" by Edgar Allan Poe

Edgar Allan Poe's "The Tell-Tale Heart" stands as a paragon of first-person narration in horror literature. The story is conveyed through the eyes of an unnamed narrator, offering an intimate glimpse into the mind of someone who commits murder and is subsequently haunted by guilt. This POV is instrumental in creating a palpable sense of paranoia and psychological turmoil. The reader is confined to the narrator's perspective, sharing in their obsessive thoughts and escalating madness, which amplifies the story's suspense and horror. The first-person narrative makes the tale's climax, where the narrator hears the beating of the dead man's heart, a deeply immersive and unsettling experience, showcasing the power of this POV in evoking visceral horror.

Second-Person POV: Rare Usage and Its Impact

The second-person POV, characterized by its direct address to the reader using "you," is a rarity in horror fiction, which makes its effective use all the more striking. While classic horror literature examples are less common, this perspective can create an unparalleled sense of immersion and complicity. In interactive horror stories or narratives aiming to breach the fourth wall, the second-person POV can place the reader in the heart of the horror, making the events and decisions feel intensely personal. Though more prevalent in modern interactive and experimental horror, the potential of the second-person POV to engage the reader directly, making them an active participant in the narrative, offers a unique avenue for horror storytelling.

Third-Person Limited POV: *The Turn of the Screw* by Henry James

Henry James's *The Turn of the Screw* exemplifies the effective use of third-person limited POV in horror, particularly within the gothic genre. The narrative unfolds primarily from the perspective of a young governess who suspects that the children in her care are being influenced by supernatural forces. This limited viewpoint is critical to the story's enduring horror, as it traps the reader within the governess's increasingly unstable perspective, creating a thick atmosphere of ambiguity and dread. The uncertainty about the reality of the ghosts—whether they are truly present or figments of the governess's imagination—serves as a central pillar of the story's horror, made possible by the constrained lens of the third-person limited POV.

Third-Person Omniscient POV: *Dracula* by Bram Stoker

Stoker's *Dracula* utilizes a third-person omniscient POV, among other narrative techniques, to craft a sweeping horror narrative that crosses geographical and character boundaries. This god-like perspective enables Stoker to present a comprehensive view of the vampire mythos, exploring the count's malevolence through various characters' experiences. The omniscient POV enriches the story, allowing for a multi-layered exploration of themes such as sexuality, invasion, and the collision of modernity with ancient superstitions. The broad scope provided by this POV amplifies the epic scale of the horror, offering readers a panoramic view of the unfolding terror and the diverse reactions of the characters involved.

Modern Horror and POV: Continuation of Classic Techniques

While focusing on classic literature, it's important to acknowledge how contemporary horror writers continue to leverage different POVs to great effect. For example, the first-person narrative in Shirley Jackson's *The Haunting of Hill House* offers a modern exploration of psychological horror, reminiscent of Poe's intimate and unreliable narrators. Similarly, Stephen King's use of third-person limited in novels like *Pet Sematary* allows for deep character exploration while maintaining suspense, echoing the techniques seen in *The Turn of the Screw*.

Through these classic and contemporary examples, the critical role of POV in horror fiction becomes evident. The chosen narrative perspective not only dictates the story's delivery but also profoundly impacts the reader's emotional journey and the overall atmosphere of the narrative. By examining these seminal works, writers can gain insights into the strategic use of POV to enhance the horror experience, making their stories resonate more deeply with readers. As we continue to explore the nuances of POV in horror writing, these examples serve as foundational touchstones, illustrating the diverse ways in which perspective can be wielded to evoke fear, suspense, and a lasting impact.

Chapter 4

Common Pitfalls and Best Practices

In crafting horror fiction, the point of view (POV) is more than a mere narrative technique. It's a conduit for the reader's experience and a framework for the story's unfolding. However, selecting and executing the POV can be fraught with challenges, and missteps in its application can detract from the horror and diminish the reader's engagement. This chapter delves into the common pitfalls associated with different POVs in horror writing, offering best practices to navigate these challenges and harness the full potential of narrative perspective.

First-Person POV: The Double-Edged Sword

The intimacy and immediacy of the first-person POV can immerse readers in the protagonist's experiences, making the horror personal and palpable. However, this closeness can also limit the narrative scope, confining the reader's knowledge to the protagonist's perspective and potentially leading to a myopic view of the story's world.

Pitfalls:

- Over-reliance on the unreliable narrator: While this trope can add layers of suspense and ambiguity, excessive or unconvincing use can frustrate readers and erode the story's credibility.

- Limited perspective: The singular viewpoint can restrict the narrative's breadth, excluding important events and character developments occurring beyond the protagonist's awareness.

Best Practices:

- Use unreliability sparingly: Employ the unreliable narrator with purpose, ensuring that the ambiguity it introduces serves the story's thematic and emotional goals.

- Expand narrative scope through other means: Incorporate letters, diary entries, or other narrative devices to provide broader context and enrich the story world.

Second-Person POV: Navigating the Uncommon Terrain

The second-person POV, with its direct address to the reader, offers a unique and immersive experience. However, its rarity and the challenge of maintaining this perspective can make it a difficult terrain to navigate in horror fiction.

Pitfalls:

- Reader alienation: The direct address can sometimes feel invasive or presumptive, potentially alienating readers who struggle to identify with the "you" being addressed.

- Narrative sustainability: Sustaining the second-person perspective over the course of a longer narrative can be challenging, risking disengagement or monotony.

Best Practices:

- Use for specific narrative effects: Reserve the second-person POV for stories where direct reader involvement is essential to the horror experience or thematic exploration.

- Mix with other POVs: Consider blending the second-person perspective with other POVs to maintain narrative momentum and variety.

Third-Person Limited POV: Balancing Focus and Flexibility

The third-person limited POV offers a balance between the intimacy of first-person and the broader scope of third-person omniscient. However, maintaining this balance while providing a comprehensive view of the story's events can be challenging.

Pitfalls:

- Inconsistent focus: Shifting too frequently between characters' perspectives can fragment the narrative and dilute the emotional impact.

- Limited information: Staying too closely aligned with one character can obscure crucial plot developments and character motivations.

Best Practices:

- Maintain consistent character focus: Choose a primary character for each section or chapter to provide a stable lens through which the story unfolds.

- Strategically reveal information: Use the protagonist's interactions with other characters and their environment to organically broaden the narrative scope.

Third-Person Omniscient POV: Mastering the God's Eye View

The third-person omniscient POV provides a panoramic view of the story's world, offering insights into multiple characters and plotlines. However, this expansive perspective can also lead to narrative diffusion and emotional distance.

Pitfalls:

- Overwhelming detail: Including too many perspectives or subplots can overwhelm the reader and dilute the central narrative thread.

- Emotional detachment: The broad viewpoint can create a distance between the reader and the characters, reducing the emotional impact of the horror.

Best Practices:

- Focus on key characters and plotlines: Prioritize the most critical perspectives and narratives to maintain clarity and momentum.

- Use close third-person passages: Temporarily narrow the focus to individual characters' thoughts and experiences to foster emotional engagement.

In navigating the challenges of POV in horror fiction, writers must strike a delicate balance between narrative scope, character development, and emotional resonance. By avoiding common pitfalls and adhering to best practices, authors can leverage the chosen POV to enhance the horror experience, deepen the reader's engagement, and craft a story that resonates with authenticity and impact. The strategic selection and execution of POV not only shapes the narrative's structure but also its soul, guiding readers through the shadows of horror with a compelling and cohesive vision.

Chapter 5

Choosing the Right POV for Your Story

The selection of the point of view (POV) is a pivotal decision in the crafting of a horror story. It influences how the narrative unfolds, how readers connect with characters, and how the horror elements are experienced. This chapter provides a guide to help writers analyze their story ideas and select the most effective POV, enhancing the narrative's impact and resonance with readers.

Analyzing Your Story

Before deciding on a POV, it's essential to consider various aspects of your story, including its themes, characters, and the type of horror you intend to explore. Ask yourself the following questions to gain clarity on the narrative's needs:

- What is the core horror element of my story? Is it psychological terror, supernatural occurrences, gothic atmosphere, or cosmic horror? Different horror elements might be better served by different POVs.

- Whose story am I telling? Is it a deeply personal journey, a shared experience among a group of characters, or a broad story involving multiple perspectives?

- What is the desired emotional impact on the reader? Do you want the reader to feel intimately connected to a single character's fear, or do you prefer to instill a sense of dread by revealing the horror from multiple viewpoints?

- How much does the reader need to know? Consider the balance between suspense and revelation. Would your story benefit from the limited knowledge of a first-person or third-person limited POV, or does it require the broader perspective of third-person omniscient?

Guiding Questions for POV Selection

Once you've analyzed the core aspects of your story, use these guiding questions to narrow down the POV choice:

- For First-Person POV: Does my story focus on the internal experience and transformation of a single character? Will exploring the narrative through their direct perspective enhance the horror and emotional depth?

- For Second-Person POV: Am I aiming to create a highly immersive experience that implicates the reader directly in the narrative? Does my story involve interactive elements or a desire to break the fourth wall?

- For Third-Person Limited POV: Do I want to maintain close proximity to my characters' thoughts and feelings while retaining the flexibility to shift focus between them? Is there a need to keep certain aspects of the horror hidden from the reader to build suspense?

- For Third-Person Omniscient POV: Does my story encompass a wide array of characters, locations, and potentially complex plotlines that require a broader perspective? Will a god-like view of the narrative world enhance the thematic exploration and horror elements?

Experimentation and Flexibility

Don't hesitate to experiment with different POVs in the early stages of your writing process. Drafting key scenes from various perspectives can provide insight into which POV most effectively conveys the horror and emotional impact of your story. Be open to changing the POV if the narrative seems to demand a different approach as it evolves. I've personally worked with several authors who had to rewrite entire manuscripts because a certain POV just didn't work in the end. Don't commit to finishing a story until you're 100% certain about the POV approach.

Encouragement to Find the Best Fit

Finding the right POV for your horror story might require time and experimentation, but it's a crucial step in crafting a narrative that resonates with readers. The chosen perspective should not only serve the plot and thematic elements but also enhance the reader's immersion and emotional engagement with the story. Remember, the POV is more than a technical choice—it's the lens through which the dark heart of your horror tale is revealed.

Selecting the POV is an integral part of the horror writing process, one that shapes the very foundation of your narrative. By carefully considering your story's needs, analyzing different perspectives, and being open to experimentation, you can choose a POV that amplifies the horror, deepens character development, and leaves a lasting impact on your readers.

Practical Exercise:

This exercise is designed to help you delve into the nuances of point of view

(POV) and its impact on your horror writing. By experimenting with different perspectives, you can gain insights into how each POV might enhance the thematic depth, emotional engagement, and horror elements of your story.

Step 1: Select a Scene

Choose a pivotal scene from your horror story. This should be a moment that is crucial to your plot and rich in emotional or horror elements—perhaps a scene of revelation, a moment of terror, or a significant character decision.

Step 2: Write in First-Person POV

Rewrite your selected scene from the first-person perspective of your protagonist or another key character. Immerse yourself in their thoughts, feelings, and sensory experiences as they navigate the scene. Consider how this intimate perspective heightens the horror and emotional impact. Reflect on the following:

- How does the first-person POV alter the reader's connection to the character and the horror they're facing?

- What new insights or tensions arise from being confined to this character's perspective?

Step 3: Experiment with Second-Person POV

Rewrite the same scene using the second-person POV. Address the reader as "you," placing them directly in the shoes of the character experiencing the horror. This perspective can be challenging but offers a unique way to engage the reader. Reflect on:

- How does the direct address change the scene's dynamics and the reader's involvement?

- Does the second-person perspective increase the immersiveness or intensity of the horror experience?

Step 4: Try Third-Person Limited POV

Now, rewrite the scene from a third-person limited perspective, focusing closely on one character's experiences and perceptions. Maintain the depth of character insight while allowing for a slight narrative distance. Consider:

- How does this perspective balance character intimacy with narrative flexibility?

- Does the third-person limited POV provide a more rounded view of the scene's events while maintaining suspense?

Step 5: Explore Third-Person Omniscient POV

Finally, approach the scene from a third-person omniscient perspective. Offer insights into multiple characters' thoughts and feelings, if applicable, and provide a broader view of the scene's context and implications. Reflect on:

- How does this god-like perspective change the storytelling scope and the layering of horror elements?

- What are the benefits and challenges of conveying the horror from this all-encompassing viewpoint?

Reflection Questions

After completing these exercises, consider the following questions to evaluate the impact of each POV on your scene and story:

- Which POV felt most natural or effective for conveying the horror in your scene? Why?

- How did each POV change the pacing, tension, and emotional depth of the scene?

- Based on this exercise, which POV do you think best serves the overall goals of your horror story?

This exercise is not just about finding the "right" POV but about understanding the narrative possibilities each perspective offers. The insights gained from experimenting with different POVs can inform your approach to storytelling, helping you to choose the perspective that most effectively brings your horror story to life. Remember, the power of horror fiction lies not just in the tale itself but in how it's told—the POV you choose is the key to unlocking this potential.

As we conclude this exploration of point of view (POV) in horror fiction, it's clear that the choice of narrative perspective is not merely a stylistic preference but a fundamental element that shapes the entire storytelling experience. Each POV, with its unique strengths and considerations, offers distinct pathways into the heart of horror, enabling writers to craft narratives that resonate deeply with readers, evoke intense emotions, and leave a lasting impression.

The journey through the various POVs—from the intimate immediacy of the first-person to the broad scope of the third-person omniscient—highlights the versatility and impact of perspective in horror writing. The first-person POV, with its direct engagement, allows readers to experience the protagonist's fear and madness up close, making the horror personal and visceral. The second-person POV, though less commonly used, offers a unique opportunity to immerse readers in the narrative, making them active participants in the unfolding terror. The third-person limited POV provides a balance, offering insight into characters' inner worlds while maintaining the suspense that is so crucial to horror. Finally, the third-person omniscient POV opens up a vast narrative landscape, allowing for a complex, multi-layered exploration of horror that can encompass multiple characters and intertwining plotlines.

Selecting the right POV for your horror story is a decision that should be informed by the narrative's thematic goals, the desired emotional impact, and the nature of the horror being explored. This choice influences not only how the story is told but also how it is experienced by the reader. The effectiveness of horror often lies in its ability to evoke empathy, fear, and suspense, and the POV is instrumental in achieving these emotional responses.

As writers, the challenge is to harness the power of POV to enhance the horror narrative, using it as a tool to deepen character development, enrich the atmosphere, and heighten the suspense. This requires not only an understanding of the strengths and limitations of each POV but also a willingness to experiment and adapt, ensuring that the chosen perspective aligns with the story's core and maximizes its impact.

In crafting your horror tales, remember that the POV is more than a lens through which the story is viewed—it is the medium through which the horror is felt, understood, and remembered. By making thoughtful, informed choices about narrative perspective, you can elevate your horror fiction, creating stories that linger in the minds of readers long after the final page is turned.

In the end, the art of horror writing is deeply connected to the power of perspective. The way you choose to tell your story—the eyes through which your readers see your world—can transform the familiar into the terrifying, the mundane into the macabre. As you venture forth into the dark realms of horror fiction, let the considerations and insights explored in these chapters guide you in selecting the POV that best serves your narrative, ensuring that your tales of terror are not only told but truly felt.

Section 4

Dialogue plays a central role in the construction of horror stories, functioning as an essential narrative device that can heighten the emotional experience and reinforce the sense of fear that is fundamental to the genre. In horror fiction, dialogue often carries a heavier burden compared to other genres. Each line must work doubly hard to advance the plot, reveal character, and most importantly, contribute to the atmosphere of dread that envelops the narrative.

To truly grasp the power of dialogue in horror, one must delve into several exemplars of classic horror literature where speech between characters is not merely a means of communication but a vessel of terror in itself.

One seminal work that demonstrates the profound impact of dialogue on the feeling of dread is Bram Stoker's *Dracula*. In the novel, the titular character's dialogue serves as a chilling indicator of his supernatural nature and malevolent intentions. An exchange that showcases this is when Dr. Van Helsing confronts Dracula. Here, the Count's words are delivered with a cold, menacing precision: "My revenge has just begun! I spread it over centuries, and time is on my side." This declaration not only cements Dracula's status as an immortal antagonist but also conveys the inexorable horror that awaits the protagonists. Stoker employs a formal, almost archaic diction for Dracula, starkly contrasting with the more conversational tone of the other characters. This linguistic juxtaposition adds to the eeriness, as it renders Dracula as an otherworldly presence among mere mortals.

Another example is found in Shirley Jackson's *The Haunting of Hill House*, where dialogue contributes to the eerie atmosphere through subtlety and ambiguity. Consider the instance when Eleanor, the protagonist, is talking to the other occupants of Hill House and hears a voice that says, "I am waiting for you." This mysterious whisper, not heard by the others, instills a creeping sense of paranoia and isolation that pervades the entire novel. Jackson uses dialogue as an unseen character; the disembodied words become a haunting presence that unnerves both Eleanor and the reader.

In H.P. Lovecraft's works, such as *The Call of Cthulhu*, dialogue is often used to convey the incomprehensibility of the ancient beings he depicts. The limited exchanges that involve these beings often include accounts from individuals who have encountered them and been driven mad by the experience. Their disjointed, frantic descriptions, although not direct speech from the entities themselves, are relayed through dialogue that paints a picture of horror beyond human understanding. Lovecraft's choice of phrasing, infused with dread and a looming sense of doom, creates an otherness that is profoundly unsettling.

Dialogue in horror also involves a strategic use of silence and what is left unsaid. In *The Woman in Black* by Susan Hill, the sparingly-used dialogue between Arthur Kipps and the inhabitants of Crythin Gifford hints at the dark secrets surrounding Eel Marsh House. Their reluctance to speak of the haunting events creates a tangible tension, with each evasion and hushed whisper serving to magnify the reader's sense of impending doom.

To make dialogue sound natural while serving the eerie atmosphere of a horror narrative, authors often utilize a technique that could be referred to as 'controlled revelation.' They withhold information deliberately, allowing characters to communicate in a way that suggests the unspeakable horrors that lie beneath the surface. These partial disclosures are more frightening than explicit descriptions, as they activate the reader's imagination to conjure up terrors that are uniquely horrifying to them.

Another technique employed is the use of dialect and idiosyncratic speech patterns. When characters speak in a manner that is particular to a specific region or group, it adds authenticity to the story's setting, and when applied effectively, this authenticity lends credibility to the supernatural elements of the plot.

Moreover, pacing in dialogue can dramatically affect the atmosphere. Rapid exchanges can build tension and a sense of urgency, while longer, more drawn-out speeches can create a slow-burning dread. Authors manipulate the rhythm of conversations to control the reader's pulse, quickening it with frenetic dialogue during scenes of chaos, and slowing it down with deliberate monologues that hint at unspeakable truths lurking in the shadows.

The power of dialogue in horror, when wielded skillfully, does not simply advance the story or develop characters; it becomes an instrument of fear. It is the unseen monster, the whisper in the dark, the promise of horrors yet to come. Through careful crafting and strategic deployment, dialogue in horror fiction becomes an echo chamber of dread, amplifying the terror that lies at the heart of the genre.

In crafting authentic dialogue in horror, writers must channel the essence of each character through their spoken words, allowing readers to experience the story through various perspectives. Authenticity in dialogue contributes significantly to the believability of the characters and, by extension, to the story's ability to induce fear and suspense. To achieve this, writers can engage in workshops that focus on developing character-specific speech patterns and utilizing subtext and silence.

Chapter 1

Dialogue formatting

These are very basic formatting examples, but you'd be surprized to see how many times we see these done wrong.

1. Commas with Dialogue Tags

When a dialogue tag follows a piece of dialogue, use a comma inside the quotation marks, and then continue the sentence outside the quotation marks with a lowercase letter (unless it's a proper noun).

Example:
"I can't believe it's already October," she said.
"Will you come with me?" he asked.

2. Periods with Action Tags

When the dialogue is followed by an action rather than a dialogue tag, use a period inside the quotation marks, and start a new sentence with a capital letter.

Example:
"We should leave now." She grabbed her coat from the chair.
"I'm not sure." He paused, looking uncertain.

3. Question Marks and Exclamation Points

Question marks and exclamation points belong inside the quotation marks when they apply to the dialogue. The dialogue tag that follows starts with a lowercase letter if it's a continuation of the sentence.

Example:
"Are you coming?" she asked.
"Never!" he exclaimed. "I won't do it."

4. Dialogue Interruptions

Use an em dash inside the quotation marks to indicate an interruption or abrupt stop in the dialogue. If the dialogue continues after an action or description, use an em dash to resume the dialogue, as well.

Example:
"I don't think you understand—"
Don't even say "he cut her off" since it's evident. Just have the next person start speaking.
"You mean you actually—" He couldn't finish his sentence, disbelief evident in his expression.

For this example, an ellipse will also work well if the dialogue just trails off.

5. Split Dialogue with Tags

When a piece of dialogue is broken up by a tag, use a comma at the end of the first part of the dialogue and after the tag. The second part of the dialogue begins with a lowercase letter unless it's the start of a new sentence.

Example:
"It's just that," she said, "I never expected it to happen this way."
"I know," he replied, "but we have to deal with it now."

OR

"I know," he replied. "Let's just get it over with."

6. Paragraphs in Dialogue

When a character's dialogue extends into multiple paragraphs, use opening quotation marks at the beginning of each paragraph, but only use closing quotation marks at the end of the final paragraph.

Example:
"I was walking through the woods. It was quiet, too quiet. I could feel something was off, but I kept going.
"Then, out of nowhere, I heard it. A low growl, unlike anything I'd ever heard. It was in that moment I knew I wasn't alone."

By adhering to these guidelines, writers can ensure their dialogue is clear and effectively communicates the intended tone and pace of the conversation. Proper formatting helps maintain the flow of the narrative and keeps the reader engaged without confusion.

Chapter 2

Talking Points: Dialogue - Scott Nicholson

Sometimes you just have to talk it out, even when you don't know what you're talking about.

That's why narrative fiction so heavily relies on dialogue. It creates conflict, gives information to the reader, moves the plot, develops the characters, and builds a sense of place. In short, it does everything, all the time, just like every element of your work should, whether it's fiction or non-fiction.

Speech denotes class, racial, cultural, educational, and geographic differences. Make sure each character speaks consistently. In real life, our grammar can change depending on the company we're keeping, but in fiction you have to keep it simple for the reader. The character who says "ain't" on page three shouldn't be saying "most certainly is not" by page 300, unless that character has gone to Harvard during the middle chapters.

Beware of dialect. When conveying dialect, a little is usually plenty. Otherwise, it becomes parody and you lose the reader. For example, your Dodge City sheriff shouldn't say, "I'm amblin' over yonder to wet muh whistle." Your Southern character shouldn't lose all the g's in her action verbs: enough "fussin' and feudin'" and your reader's eyesight will blur. Use colloquialisms in moderation, and let your grammar do most of the work instead of relying on tics, tricks, and dropped letters. "We don't have no pumpkins," or "We ain't got no pumpkins" is fine, but make sure all the characters don't talk alike. And you might need to only drop the effect once or twice to plant the idea in the reader's mind.

In my novel The Manor, I have a minor character who is a Southern belle. She is educated, and therefore I simply said she was from the South and didn't attempt to drench her with slang, moonshine, and magnolias. In fact, the only direct reference to her accent is when she is mocked by her lover: "Why don't ya'll get yosef gone with the wind?" She never actually says "ya'll" herself. I know Southern speech patterns fairly well, and much of the effect is oral rather than literal. It's not just Southerners who drop the g in –ing words, and they're not doing it because they're dumb, shiftless, and lazy. In fact, much of the Appalachian speech often seen as backwoods and backward ("I'm afixin' to feed the chickens") is the remnant of very formal Celtic speech that crossed the Atlantic several hundred years ago.

In the same novel, I have a character who has adopted a fake British accent because he wants to appear classy. He's atrocious and almost a parody. He says things like, "Bloody hell," and "Righty right," and a lot of the little phrases you hear in movies like "Shaun of the Dead" and "The Full Monty." It works because that's where he "learned" his accent. If I had used a real British character, I would have had to work much harder, because most of my exposure to British speech is through movies and the occasional book, which can't be fully trusted to convey authentic speech.

I am not a huge Lovecraft fan, and I think a lot of it has to do with his attempts to tag rural New England dialect. "Ye can have ye're money back. I don't want truck with any kin o' Septimus Bishop. It's jest aoutside my door. Snufflin' araoun.'" Lovecraft's educated characters display few distinctive speech patterns. It's lazy, it's classist, it's just plain bad writing, Lovecraft's unique ideas aside.

For the opposite reason, I love Elmore Leonard's work. Somehow even his nasty characters seem to have a dignity about them. This is from the mouth of a black houseman: "Mmmm, that musta impressed him. Yeah, Jacktown have riots and everything up there. What the man likes is to rub against danger without getting any on him. Make him feel like a macho man. You know what I'm saying?" To me, this reflects a streetwise voice but one that is not generic. The line about rubbing against danger makes it smart and Leonard doesn't have to diminish his black character with, "You sho' got that right, homey."

It's not only spoken dialogue that can create pitfalls. Internal dialogue, and even the point-of-view voice, must ring true. There's a great line by mystery writer Margaret Maron: "I is not me." Your first-person fictional character doesn't have to speak the way you do. If you are writing your autobiography, then your voice will emerge, but even then your "writing voice" will be different from your speaking voice. For example, a large number of people add the "th" sound to the end of "height" when they say it, which is plain stupid, but it would be even stupider if you spelled it "heighth" in your dialogue.

Most modern novels feature third-person limited viewpoints, meaning the reader gets into the character's head and views the world through his or her eyes. This allows you to make the most of internal dialogue. I don't know about you, but I talk to myself a lot inside my own head. That voice is different than what I would be saying if I were actually using my tongue. And if you let your characters talk to you, chances are good they will emerge with their own individual voices and rhythms.

You can read pieces of your dialogue aloud to make sure they work for the ear, but remember that written dialogue functions differently than actual speech. It doesn't have to be real, because real speech is filled with ums, ers, and utter banalities. Don't let a character ask about the weather unless you're writing a natural-disaster thriller. Even if you're writing non-fiction and using actual quotes, you'll still have to decide which sentences are of interest and value. Most of all, make sure there's a reason your characters are saying what they are saying, and pay attention to how they are saying it. There's enough hot air and blabber in the world already.

Scott Nicholson is the author of THEY HUNGER, THE FARM, THANK YOU FOR THE FLOWERS, *and four other novels. He's a professional freelance editor, an organic gardener, a semi-professional liar, and a goat breeder. His website www.hauntedcomputer.com serves up a blog and more writing advice.*

Chapter 3

Character-Specific Speech Patterns

Character-specific speech patterns involve creating a distinct voice for each character that reflects their background, personality, and current emotional state. These patterns are vital in differentiating characters and adding depth to their interactions. To practice this technique, writers can engage in the following exercises:

- Character Interviews: Write a series of interview questions and answer them as your characters. This helps in understanding their speech idiosyncrasies, such as whether they use formal language, slang, or have a specific dialect. Pay attention to the rhythm and vocabulary they use, which should align with their personality and backstory.

- Dialogue Switch: Take a piece of dialogue and rewrite it for different characters, observing how the language changes with each new speaker. This sharpens the ability to differentiate each character's voice.

- Emotional Monologues: Focus on a single character and write a monologue that captures their emotional response to a horror scenario. Monitor how their speech pattern changes with their emotions, noting shifts in pitch, pace, and choice of words.

- Group Dynamics: Write a scene with multiple characters engaging in conversation. Practice orchestrating the flow of dialogue, ensuring that each character's contribution reflects their individual speech pattern and how they react to one another.

Subtext and Silence

Subtext is the underlying meaning behind the words spoken by characters. In horror, subtext can be used to communicate unspoken fears or tensions between characters. Silence, on the other hand, can be just as telling, creating suspense or emphasizing the unsaid. To explore these tools, writers can utilize the following exercises:

- Subtext Scenarios: Write a dialogue-heavy scene where characters speak about mundane things while an undercurrent of horror looms. The exercise should focus on infusing subtext that hints at the underlying dread without explicitly stating it.

- The Unspoken: Write a scene where the main conflict or horror element is never directly mentioned in dialogue. Characters should dance around the topic, and the writer must convey the gravity of the situation through subtext and characters' reactions.

- Silent Tension: Craft a scene where silence is a character in its own right. Characters may pause before speaking, or there may be moments where no words are necessary, allowing the reader to sense the fear and tension through described actions and reactions.

- Reveal Through Concealment: Compose a dialogue in which a character is hiding something. The goal is to have the reader understand what is being concealed through what is said, how it's said, and what is purposely left out.

- The Loaded Question: Create an exercise where one character must ask another a question that has a significant subtext. The other character's response, whether through words or silence, should reveal their awareness of the subtext and contribute to the eerie atmosphere.

By practicing these exercises, writers will learn to give each character a unique voice that resonates within the horror narrative. They will also master the art of conveying deeper meanings and stirring emotions through what characters say or choose not to say. The dialogue becomes not just a vessel for communication but a layered storytelling element that enriches the horror experience.

Authentic dialogue is a dance between the said and the unsaid, the explicit and the implicit. In the realm of horror, it is where the unseen is suggested, and the unspeakable is intimated, heightening the sense of fear and anticipation. Through disciplined practice and a keen understanding of their characters' psyches, writers can craft dialogue that is both authentic and chilling, enhancing the overall impact of the horror story.

Internal monologue serves as an intimate bridge connecting readers to a character's inner world, a space where fears, desires, and secrets lurk in the shadows, often more frightening than the overt horrors that manifest externally. In horror fiction, the artful integration of a character's thoughts can be as vital to the atmosphere and suspense as the eerie setting or the lurking antagonist. To guide horror writers in weaving internal monologue into their tales, we must explore techniques that are both subtle and powerful, crafting thought processes that not only reveal character depth but also amplify the story's tension and psychological impact.

Chapter 4
Internal Monologue

An effective internal monologue should serve a distinct purpose within the narrative. It might provide insight into a character's motivation, reveal a backstory that sheds light on their current fears, or offer readers a glimpse of the character's emotional response to the unfolding horror. Crucially, it should feel organic, seamlessly blending with the character's perspective and the larger narrative.

Example of Effective Use:

Imagine a scene where the protagonist hears a faint whisper from the attic in an otherwise silent house. An effective internal monologue might delve into their trepidation:

"That sound again—like words brushed across sandpaper. It's impossible, isn't it? Dad sealed the attic years ago after what happened to Mom. Still, every rational thought pales against the ice-cold dread curling around my spine. Something is up there—something or someone, whispering my name."

This internal dialogue effectively increases suspense by reflecting the protagonist's fear and curiosity while teasing the reader with hints about a tragic past event connected to the attic. It also exemplifies how internal monologue can offer context and deepen the narrative without needing expository dialogue.

Ineffective Use and Its Consequences

Conversely, ineffective internal monologue can disrupt the pacing, confuse readers, or even dissipate tension if it delves into unnecessary tangents or over-explains the protagonist's thoughts.

Example of Ineffective Use:

Consider the same scenario with a less effective internal monologue:

"I wonder what that noise is? It sounds like a whisper, but that can't be right. Maybe it's just the wind. Then again, it could be a rat, or perhaps the house is just old and making noises. Mom didn't like the attic. I remember she was always worried about it before she passed away. I wonder if it's going to rain tomorrow?"

Here, the internal monologue meanders, touching on irrelevant details that neither build character nor advance the plot. The inclusion of the mother's opinion on the attic feels disconnected from the immediate horror, and the abrupt shift to thoughts about the weather further diminishes the scene's tension.

Heightening Suspense with Internal Monologue

To use internal monologue as a tool for heightening suspense, writers must be acutely aware of timing and placement. Thoughts can be interspersed with action to punctuate moments of high tension or used to build anticipation before a terrifying event. They should be like the quiet before the storm—a space filled with anxiety and portent.

Consider an example where the protagonist is about to enter a basement where a malevolent presence is rumored to dwell. An internal monologue that mirrors the protagonist's mounting dread can enhance the suspense exponentially:

"With every step toward that door, the heaviness in the air magnifies. Why am I doing this? To prove I'm not afraid? But I am—terrified. They say evil has a scent, and now, at the threshold, I understand. It smells like decay and feels like the weight of a thousand stares. Do I dare pull back the veil between our world and its?"

This internal questioning reflects the protagonist's fear while inviting readers to share in the trepidation. The description of an evil scent and the weight of stares creates an immersive sensory experience, setting the stage for the horrors that may lie ahead.

Techniques for Integrating Internal Monologue

Several techniques can be employed to ensure that internal monologue adds to the horror narrative without detracting from it:

- Concise and sporadic: Keep internal thoughts concise and sporadic to prevent them from bogging down the narrative. They should act as seasoning, not overshadow the main course of action and dialogue.

- Immediate and present: Write internal monologue in the present tense, even if the rest of the narrative is past tense, to give a sense of immediacy and engagement with the character's current state of mind.

- Relevance: Ensure that every internal thought reveals something relevant about the character or their situation. If it doesn't serve the story or the atmosphere, it should be cut.

- Psychological authenticity: Delve into the authentic and raw psychological state of characters facing terror. Let readers feel the panic, confusion, or resolve that drives the character forward in the story.

- Contrast and conflict: Use internal monologue to create contrast between what a character shows externally and what they are truly feeling or thinking, adding layers to the character and creating conflict that drives the narrative.

Balancing Internal Monologue with Action

Too much introspection can slow a story's pace, while too little can leave characters feeling shallow. This chapter discusses strategies for striking the right balance between action and internal monologue to maintain tension and propel the plot.

The delicate dance between action and internal monologue is akin to a carefully choreographed ballet—the movement and stillness must be in perfect harmony to create a performance that captivates the audience. Horror, as a genre that thrives on pacing and suspense, necessitates a mastery of this balance to maintain narrative momentum while providing characters with depth and realism. Writers must, therefore, learn to identify key moments that warrant reflection, and others that demand action. Below are exercises designed to sharpen this skill and infuse the tale with the seamless coexistence of introspection and movement.

Exercise 1: The Mirror Scene

Start by writing a scene that features a character looking into a mirror in an eerie setting. Mirrors in horror often symbolize self-examination, hidden truths, and occasionally, portals to other dimensions. Describe the character's appearance and have them notice something unsettling. This is where action begins—perhaps a shadow flits across the glass, or their reflection blinks out of sync.

Immediately follow with internal monologue. What does the character think about this anomaly? How do they rationalize it? Instead of allowing the character to ruminate for paragraphs, intersperse their thought with action. Maybe they reach out to touch the mirror, only for it to ripple like water. Their thoughts should be fragmented, mimicking the staccato of their startled heart.

This exercise teaches the value of reflection in moments of stillness and the necessity of swift action following a disturbing revelation, while keeping the reader engaged and the pace steady.

Exercise 2: The Haunting Past

Develop a scene where the protagonist is forced to confront a location from their past—a childhood home, an abandoned school, or a neglected graveyard. Begin with descriptive action, the approach to the place, the creak of a gate, the crunch of leaves underfoot.

After the initial description, bring in the internal monologue. Have the protagonist recall a memory tied to the location, one that is brief yet significant. Once the memory surfaces, pull back into action. Perhaps an unexplained sound or a sudden change in the environment occurs.

The aim here is to use internal monologue to imbue the setting with personal horror before snapping the reader back to the immediacy of the character's situation. It's a lesson in pacing the ebb and flow of action and introspection to maximize impact.

Exercise 3: The Descent into Madness

In this exercise, write a sequence where the protagonist is losing their grip on reality. Begin with a series of chaotic actions—running from an unseen threat, wildly turning in circles, gasping for breath. These vivid physical actions set a frenetic pace.

Transition into the internal monologue as the character attempts to understand their unraveling senses. Let their thoughts spiral, but not too far or long before a sudden noise or a jarring physical sensation pulls them back to the present.

Here, the task is to simulate the disorientation of fear, blending the character's internal chaos with external stimulus. It teaches the importance of using internal monologue to offer insight into a character's psyche without stalling the action.

Exercise 4: The Creature Reveal

Craft a scene introducing a monstrous entity. Describe the creature's emergence into the scene with gripping action, noting the protagonist's physical reactions—stumbling backward, a gasp, the dropping of an object.

Follow with internal monologue, but keep it tight. What is the shock of the encounter? Is there recognition, or is the beast beyond comprehension? The character's internal response should be instinctual, primal, and brief, reflecting a mind in survival mode.

This exercise trains the writer to insert quick bursts of internal monologue in between beats of action to maintain tension and reader engagement during critical scenes.

Exercise 5: The Decision Point

Write about a character's critical choice—whether to open a door, to confront a ghost, or to delve deeper into the unknown. Start with their hand on the doorknob or foot poised to step forward, a moment of hesitation laden with action potential.

Introduce the internal monologue as they weigh their options. Let this be a moment of deep introspection that reveals character motivation and backstory. However, just as the thoughts threaten to overtake the scene, force the decision into action—perhaps the door swings open on its own, or a voice calls out, compelling the character to move.

The exercise serves to show how contemplative moments can culminate in significant, plot-driving actions. It is about understanding the rhythm of hesitation and resolve, the interplay of thought and movement.

Exercise 6: The Silent Witness

Envision a scene where the protagonist observes something horrific—a ritual, a transformation, or a silent scream. Have them hide and witness with detailed action the horrors before them.

Shift into their internal monologue as they process the event. This introspection should come in whispers, interspersed with descriptions of the continuing horror before their eyes—offering a real-time reaction that doesn't distract from the action.

The writer learns from this exercise how to balance description and reflection, ensuring that the narrative doesn't lose its sense of immediacy even while the character's thoughts add depth and horror to the unfolding event.

Exercise 7: The Lull Before The Storm

Design a scene that is the calm before an anticipated horror—the protagonist waiting in the dark, the silence in a haunted house, the stillness in the woods. Begin with their physical stillness and the absence of action, a deceptive peace.

Introduce their internal monologue as they reflect on the situation. Yet, as they descend into their thoughts, cut the monologue short with a startling action—a sudden noise, a shift in the environment, or the onset of an actual storm.

This teaches pacing by balancing the quiet moments of dread-filled antici-pation with the sharp onset of terror, demonstrating the interplay of internal reflection with the action that drives a horror narrative forward.

Each exercise is designed to fine-tune the writer's sense of pacing, teaching how to wield internal monologue and action in tandem to create a horror story that is both contemplative and compelling. Through practice, writers will learn to recognize the opportune moments for a character's internal voice to take the stage and when to allow action to drive the terror home.

When crafting a horror narrative, the internal monologue is a crucial element that can be used to breathe life into a character, allowing readers to delve into the deepest recesses of their psyche, experiencing their fears, doubts, and desires. This vivid introspection not only adds depth to characters but also ratchets up the tension, making for a more immersive and terrifying read. Let's examine the internal monologues of iconic horror characters and explore the techniques that make them hauntingly compelling.

Iconic Horror Character: Jack Torrance - *The Shining*

In Stephen King's *The Shining*, Jack Torrance's descent into madness is in-tricately portrayed through his internal monologue. King masterfully presents Jack's thoughts in a fragmented and chaotic manner as his grip on sanity loosens. He uses the Overlook Hotel's influence and Jack's own vulnerabilities to demonstrate how internal dialogue can mirror the crumbling state of a char-acter's mind. Jack's thoughts often swing between his love for his family and the violent urges instilled by the hotel, reflecting the duality of his character.

Writing Prompt:
Begin by establishing your character's primary internal conflict.

Write a series of internal monologues that grow increasingly disjointed as external pressures compound their fears.

Reflect the character's environment in their thoughts, letting the setting seep into their psyche.

Iconic Horror Character: Clarice Starling - *The Silence of the Lambs*

Clarice Starling's internal monologue is a blend of her strong desire to catch the killer and her past traumas. Thomas Harris uses her introspection to reveal her motivations and the underlying insecurities that stem from her childhood. Her thoughts often reflect a keen analytical mind battling with vulnerability, making her a layered and relatable protagonist.

Writing Prompt:

Write from the point of view of a character hunting a killer.

Use internal monologue to convey their analytical process and the emotional toll of their task.

Intersperse their logic-driven thoughts with flashbacks to a formative event that shapes their resolve.

Iconic Horror Character: Carrie White - *Carrie*

In *Carrie*, Stephen King allows readers to see the world through Carrie White's eyes, whose internal monologues reveal her loneliness and despair. Her thoughts are imbued with the pain of bullying and the fear of her own powers. King's use of internal dialogue accentuates Carrie's isolation and the explosive nature of her suppressed emotions.

Writing Prompt:

Center your narrative on a character with a terrifying ability they do not fully understand.

Through internal monologue, explore their feelings of isolation and confusion.

Culminate in a pivotal moment where their emotions and powers intertwine in a critical event.

Iconic Horror Character: Eleanor Vance - *The Haunting of Hill House*

Shirley Jackson's Eleanor Vance is an excellent study of a character whose internal monologue blurs the lines between reality and fantasy. Eleanor's musings reveal her longing for belonging and her susceptibility to Hill House's hauntings. Jackson showcases a mastery of internal dialogue that gradually unveils the character's unraveling sanity.

Writing Prompt:

Construct a character who is susceptible to the supernatural.

Use their internal monologue to cast doubt on what is real and what is imagined.

Weave between lucidity and confusion, ending each monologue with a chilling ambiguity.

Iconic Horror Character: Dr. Frankenstein - *Frankenstein*

Mary Shelley's Dr. Victor Frankenstein provides a classic example of a character whose internal dialogue oscillates between the thrill of scientific discovery and the horror of his creation. His monologues explore the themes of responsibility, guilt, and the search for redemption. Shelley gives voice to the torment that haunts Frankenstein, providing a cautionary tale of ambition run amok.

Writing Prompt:
Imagine a character who has gone beyond societal bounds in their pursuit of knowledge.

Craft internal monologues that capture their initial triumph and growing despair as the consequences of their actions unfold.

Lead to a moment of profound reckoning, juxtaposing their dreams with their nightmare reality.

The examination of these iconic internal monologues reveals several key elements that contribute to their effectiveness: the use of fragmented thoughts to depict mental instability, a reflective tone that communicates depth and vulnerability, and the alignment of the character's internal struggles with external conflicts. By interlacing fears, motivations, and background stories, these monologues become powerful tools that serve to deepen the horror and engage the reader on a more intimate level.

To harness the power of internal monologue in your own horror writing, consider the following prompts designed to help you experiment with different techniques. Use these exercises to explore your characters' inner worlds, to create tension, and to propel your story forward with an authentic and terrifying voice.

Chapter 5

Checklist for Reviewing Dialogue and Internal Monologue

1. Authenticity in Voice:

- Ensure each character's dialogue is distinct and consistent with their backstory and personality.

- Check for modern phrases in period pieces or anachronisms that break immersion.

- Verify that characters react realistically to terrifying situations, with their speech reflecting appropriate emotional responses.

2. Exposition and Subtext:

- Avoid using dialogue for heavy exposition that could be better revealed through action or descriptive prose.

- Aim for subtext, where characters say one thing but mean another, to add layers to interactions.

- Assess if the dialogue indirectly reveals necessary information without being overt.

3. Brevity and Impact:

- Trim redundant dialogue that doesn't serve character development or plot advancement.

- Evaluate if the dialogue has a punch—every line should have a purpose, especially in horror.

- Refine exchanges to heighten tension, especially in scenes leading up to a scare or revelation.

4. Internal Consistency:

- Compare dialogue to ensure it doesn't contradict previous character knowledge or established facts.

- Check internal monologues for consistency in the character's thought process and worldview.

- Revisit your narrative to confirm that characters' internal conflicts are reflected in their dialogue.

5. Avoiding Melodrama:

- Sidestep overly dramatic or clichéd lines that can detract from the horror atmosphere.

- Use restraint in characters' internal reactions to avoid melodramatic overthinking.

- Maintain a balance between dialogue and silent moments to let the horror elements breathe.

6. Show vs. Tell:

- Show the character's fear and thought process through their actions and interactions, not just through their thoughts.

- Double-check that internal monologues enhance the narrative instead of explaining what the reader already knows.

- Use dialogue to show relationships and tensions between characters without explicitly telling the reader.

7. Pacing and Rhythm:

- Analyze the rhythm of dialogue to ensure it matches the pacing of the scene.

- In internal monologues, vary sentence lengths to reflect the character's emotional state and maintain reader interest.

- Ensure that dialogue isn't slowing down important action sequences, unless it's a deliberate choice to build suspense.

8. Use of Silence and Pause:

- Utilize silence and pauses effectively in dialogue to amplify horror elements.

- Review if internal monologue pauses at critical moments to increase suspense.

- Ensure that silence is used as a tool for tension, not as filler or lack of content.

9. Psychological Depth:

- Ensure internal monologues reveal deeper fears, insecurities, or motivations that align with the character's psyche.

- Check that dialogue subtly conveys the psychological underpinnings of each character.

- Revise internal monologues to peel back layers of the character, rather than stating the obvious.

10. Alignment with Theme and Atmosphere:

- Validate that both dialogue and internal monologue reinforce the story's themes.

- Adapt the characters' spoken and internal language to fit the atmospheric needs of the horror genre.

- Reflect the eeriness, dread, or chaos of the setting through the characters' word choices and thoughts.

Chapter 6

Integrating Narrative with Dialogue and Internal Monologue

In crafting compelling horror fiction, the seamless integration of narrative exposition with dialogue and internal monologue is crucial. This chapter will explore strategies for blending these elements to create a rich, immersive reading experience that maintains tension, develops characters, and advances the plot without sacrificing pace or atmosphere.

The Dance of Narrative and Dialogue

Narrative and dialogue in fiction often perform a delicate dance, where each element complements the other to build a cohesive and engaging story. Here's how to harmonize them:

- Advance the Plot through Dialogue: Use dialogue to reveal key plot points and information organically, avoiding the need for lengthy narrative exposition. This keeps the story moving and maintains reader interest.

   Example: Instead of narrating the history of a haunted house, have characters discuss rumors or personal experiences related to it in their conversations.

- Use Narrative to Set the Scene for Dialogue: Before a significant conversation, use narrative to establish the setting, mood, and stakes. This context enriches the dialogue, making it more impactful.

  Example: Describe the eerie silence and oppressive atmosphere of an abandoned asylum before characters discuss their plan to investigate it.

Weaving Internal Monologue with Narrative

Internal monologue offers a glimpse into a character's psyche, providing depth and relatability. Here's how to blend it with the narrative:

- Reflect on Actions and Dialogue: After a pivotal action or piece of dialogue, use the character's internal monologue to reflect on the event, offering insight into their thoughts and feelings. This adds layers to the narrative and deepens character development.

  Example: Following a tense encounter with a supernatural entity, the protagonist's internal monologue can reveal their fear, skepticism, or determination, providing a personal perspective on the events.

- Use Internal Monologue to Foreshadow: Sprinkle hints and foreshadowing about future plot developments within a character's thoughts. This builds suspense and keeps readers engaged, wondering how these forebodings will unfold.

  Example: A character might internally express an ominous feeling about a particular location or artifact, hinting at its significance in the story.

Balancing Narrative Exposition

While narrative exposition is necessary for background information and setting description, it's important to balance it with dialogue and internal monologue. Here's how:

- Break Up Exposition with Dialogue: Intersperse explanatory passages with dialogue to keep the narrative dynamic and prevent information overload. Dialogue can also offer different perspectives on the exposition, adding depth.

  Example: In the midst of describing an ancient curse, characters might debate its origins and effects, breaking up the exposition and introducing varying viewpoints.

- Reveal Background Information Gradually: Instead of front-loading the narrative with background details, reveal them gradually through dialogue and internal thoughts as they become relevant to the story. This maintains mystery and reader curiosity.

  Example: Details about a character's tragic past might emerge slowly, through snippets of dialogue and fleeting thoughts, as the story progresses.

Practical Exercises

- Dialogue-Narrative Integration: Write a scene where a character learns about a significant plot point through dialogue. Then, use the narrative to show the setting and the character's non-verbal reactions.

- Internal Monologue Reflection: Choose a scene with a critical action or revelation. Write an internal monologue for a character reflecting on this event, weaving in their personal fears, hopes, or secrets.

By mastering the integration of narrative, dialogue, and internal monologue, writers can create a rich tapestry of horror fiction that captivates readers, immersing them fully in the chilling world they've crafted.

Chapter 7

Revision Strategies for Refining Narrative Voice

By rigorously applying the checks below and utilizing these revision strategies, you can elevate your horror stories, ensuring that every line of dialogue and thought contributes to an atmosphere of dread and unease. A careful review, paired with strategic revision, will result in a narrative that not only tells a terrifying tale but does so with a voice that is hauntingly authentic and compelling.

- Read Aloud: Hearing the dialogue and internal monologue can highlight unnatural phrasing or pacing issues.

- Peer Feedback: Share your work with others to see if the dialogue and internal monologue have the intended effect and are free from the common pitfalls.

- Character Studies: Write additional character backstories and interactions outside the story's plot to better understand their voice.

- Scene Reimagining: Rewrite scenes from different characters' perspectives to ensure the dialogue and internal monologue remain true to each character.

- Restructure: Sometimes the order of scenes or exchanges can affect the impact of dialogue and internal monologue. Rearrange to find the most effective structure.

- Highlighting: Color-code dialogue and thoughts to ensure a balance and variety in the narrative voice.

- Streamlining: Remove any dialogue or internal monologue that doesn't serve the story's horror element or character development.

- Subtext Enhancement: Revisit dialogue to imbue it with double meanings or hidden layers that contribute to the suspense and horror.

- Silence Insertion: Intentionally add moments of silence to give weight to the dialogue and internal monologue, allowing the horror to resonate more deeply.

Chapter 8

Practical Exercises for Horror Dialogue and Monologue

To master the use of dialogue and internal monologue in horror fiction, it is essential to engage in targeted practice. The following exercises are crafted to refine your narrative voice and enhance the haunting atmosphere in your storytelling.

Exercise 1: Character Voice Differentiation
Objective: Develop distinct character voices to add realism to your dialogue.

Choose two or three characters from your work-in-progress or create new ones for this exercise. Write a scene where these characters are trapped in a tense situation (e.g., hiding from a malevolent entity). Each character should speak at least five lines of dialogue. Focus on how their word choices, sentence structures, and speech rhythms reflect their personalities and backgrounds. After finishing, read the dialogue aloud and adjust any lines that sound too similar between characters.

Exercise 2: The Subtext Game
Objective: Craft dialogue rich in subtext to add depth to your horror narrative.

Write a conversation between two characters where one knows a terrifying secret the other does not. The character with the secret must communicate with the other without revealing the secret explicitly. Aim for at least ten exchanges where the subtext is clear to the reader but not to the other character. This will help you practice implying more than what is said on the surface, creating tension and intrigue.

Exercise 3: Dialogue Reduction
Objective: Create impactful dialogue by eliminating the unnecessary.

Select a dialogue-heavy scene from an existing work or draft a new one. Identify and highlight lines that are repetitive, provide unnecessary information, or do not serve the advancement of the plot or characters. Cut these lines and rework the scene to be as concise as possible while maintaining clarity and emotional impact. This will train you to write dialogue that is sharp and purpose-driven.

Exercise 4: Internal Consistency Challenge
Objective: Ensure the dialogue is consistent with character development and plot.

Review a scene with significant dialogue. Check the consistency of each character's statements with their previously established knowledge, beliefs, and experiences. Rewrite any inconsistent lines to align with the character's personality and backstory. This exercise emphasizes the need for characters to remain true to themselves, which is crucial for reader engagement.

Exercise 5: Non-verbal Communication Practice
Objective: Convey emotions and reactions through actions, not words.

Choose a scene that relies heavily on dialogue to express fear or suspense.

Rewrite the scene, reducing the dialogue by half, and instead use characters' actions or body language to communicate the same emotions and reactions. This exercise will help you show rather than tell, which is a powerful tool in horror writing.

Exercise 6: Crafting Fears through Internal Monologue
Objective: Use internal monologue to explore and expose a character's deepest fears.

Write an internal monologue for a character experiencing a terrifying event, focusing on their raw and immediate thoughts. Use fragmented sentences, rhetorical questions, and sensory details to convey their fear. Aim for a monologue that gradually reveals the character's deepest insecurities or phobias related to the event, deepening the horror effect for the reader.

Exercise 7: Rhythm and Pacing Variation
Objective: Match the rhythm of dialogue and internal monologue to the pacing of a horror scene.

Select a scene where the pacing is crucial (e.g., a chase or the moments before a character makes a horrifying discovery). Write the dialogue and internal monologue paying close attention to sentence length, punctuation, and paragraph breaks to create a rhythm that complements the scene's pacing. Short, choppy sentences can increase tension, while longer ones can build suspense.

Exercise 8: Silence and Pause in Dialogue
Objective: Amplify horror elements by effectively incorporating silence and pauses.

Revise a scene to include strategic silences or pauses in the dialogue. Identify moments where a character would realistically be too afraid to speak or would need to stop to listen for something frightening. Insert pauses or beats into the scene where they enhance the atmosphere of dread, and remove unnecessary chatter to let the horror elements stand out.

Exercise 9: Revealing Psychological Depth
Objective: Use internal monologue to reveal psychological depth without stating the obvious.

Write an internal monologue for a character who is slowly realizing the horror of their situation. Avoid overtly stating what they are thinking; instead, use their perception of their environment, reactions to stimuli, and visceral feelings to show their state of mind. This exercise will train you to convey psychological depth subtly, creating a more immersive experience.

Exercise 10: Theme and Atmosphere Alignment
Objective: Align dialogue and internal monologue with the story's horror themes.

Select a theme or motif from your horror story and rewrite a scene, ensuring that every line of dialogue and thought from the internal monologue ties back to that theme. Use language, imagery, and metaphors that reflect the theme and contribute to the atmosphere you want to create. This exercise will help you maintain thematic cohesion throughout your narrative.

Exercise 11: Internal Monologue and Action Balance
Objective: Find a balance between action and internal monologue that maintains tension.

Take a scene with a mix of action and internal monologue. Rewrite the scene, experimenting with the placement and length of internal thoughts to ensure they do not disrupt the action. Intersperse thoughts with sensory details and actions to keep the reader grounded in the scene. Adjust until you find the balance that sustains the horror and keeps the pace taut.

Exercise 12: Strengthening Subtext Through Revision
Objective: Enhance subtext in dialogue to contribute to suspense and horror.

Revise a conversation between characters in your story, aiming to add layers of meaning. Replace direct statements with ones that imply more than they say, and hint at hidden fears or secrets. Ensure that the subtext serves the dual purpose of deepening character relationships and adding to the horror atmosphere.

Exercise 13: Embracing Unreliable Narrators in Internal Monologue
Objective: Craft internal monologues that cast doubt on the reliability of the narrator.

Compose an internal monologue from the perspective of an unreliable narrator. This character may misinterpret events, deny reality, or be influenced by paranoia. Use their internal monologue to cast doubt on what the reader has been led to believe, creating a sense of uncertainty and unease that is central to effective horror writing.

Exercise 14: Streamlining Dialogue and Monologue
Objective: Streamline dialogue and internal monologue to heighten horror.

Review a section of your story, looking for areas where dialogue or internal monologue can be shortened or simplified. Rewrite these sections, focusing on economy of language and removing any fluff. The goal is to make every word count, with each line of dialogue and thought contributing to the rising horror in the story.

Exercise 15: Reflective Writing for Psychological Depth
Objective: Use reflective writing exercises to explore characters' inner fears.

Select a character and spend ten minutes writing free-form from their perspective, delving into their deepest fears and anxieties. Do not worry about grammar or coherence; the aim is to tap into the raw emotion and psychological complexity of the character. Afterward, look for insights that can be woven into the character's internal monologue in your story to give it greater psychological depth.

By engaging with these exercises, you will refine your skills in creating dialogue and internal monologue that not only propels the plot but also resonates with the essence of horror, intensifying the emotional and psychological stakes of your narrative. These practices, when applied diligently, can transform your writing into a vessel that delivers unforgettable horror experiences to readers.

Section 5

Revision and Editing

Chapter 1

Structural Edits

In the realm of horror fiction, where the boundary between the known and the unknown blurs, structural edits serve as the backbone of your narrative, ensuring that the tale you weave holds not just coherence but also an unyielding grip on your readers' fears and imaginations. This chapter delves into the crucial aspects of structural editing, focusing on plot consistency and pacing, character development, setting and atmosphere, and the integration of themes and symbolism.

Plot Consistency and Pacing

A well-crafted horror story is like a meticulously designed maze; every twist and turn is deliberate, guiding the reader through a journey of suspense, surprise, and, inevitably, to the heart of terror. To achieve this, your plot must unfold logically, each scene building upon the last to escalate the tension and horror.

- Review Plot Structure: Begin by outlining your story's major plot points. Ensure that each event leads naturally to the next, with no logical gaps that might jolt the reader out of the story.

- Manage Pacing: Pacing is the rhythm of your narrative. Too fast, and you risk glossing over moments that could heighten suspense; too slow, and the dread might seep away. Use shorter, sharper sentences to quicken the pace during moments of high tension and longer, more descriptive passages to build atmosphere and suspense.

Character Development

In horror fiction, characters are not merely players. They are the lenses through which we experience fear. Their development is pivotal, as readers must believe in their journey to feel the terror that stalks them.

- Consistency and Depth: Ensure your characters act consistently according to their developed traits and backgrounds. A character's actions under duress can reveal deeper layers of their psyche, adding depth and realism.

- Motivations and Actions: Every action your characters take should stem from clear motivations, contributing to their arc and the story's progression. Inconsistencies here can weaken the narrative's believability.

Setting and Atmosphere

The setting in horror fiction is more than a backdrop. It's an active participant in the story, imbued with the power to evoke fear. It's the creaking floorboards, the chilling wind, the oppressive darkness—all elements that contribute to the horror atmosphere.

- Vivid Descriptions: Ensure your settings are vividly described to immerse the reader fully. Use sensory details to bring scenes to life, allowing readers to feel the cold mist, smell the decay, and hear the distant, unsettling sounds.

- Atmosphere: The setting should also reflect and enhance the story's mood. An abandoned asylum, a fog-shrouded forest, or a claustrophobic cabin in the woods - each should be described in a way that amplifies the horror and reflects the story's thematic undertones.

Theme and Symbolism

Themes and symbols enrich your narrative, adding layers of meaning that resonate with readers on a deeper level. In horror, they can be particularly potent, tapping into universal fears and the dark aspects of human nature.

- Integration of Themes: Identify the central themes of your story, whether it's the fragility of sanity, the inevitability of death, or the fear of the unknown. Ensure that these themes are woven throughout the narrative, influencing plot developments, character arcs, and setting choices.

- Use of Symbolism: Symbols can serve as shorthand for complex ideas, adding depth to your story without the need for lengthy exposition. A decaying house might symbolize the protagonist's deteriorating mind, or a persistent fog could represent the characters' murky understanding of the truth. Review your use of symbols to ensure they're consistent and meaningful, enhancing the narrative rather than distracting from it.

Structural edits demand a bird's-eye view of your manuscript, a willingness to dissect and reconstruct, and an eye for the minutiae that contribute to the narrative's overall impact. By ensuring plot consistency and pacing, you maintain the story's logical flow and suspense. Through careful character development, you create a conduit for the reader's fear. The setting and atmosphere envelop the reader in the story's mood, while themes and symbols add a rich layer of meaning. Together, these elements form the skeleton of your horror story, a framework that supports and enhances the terror within. In the revision process, addressing these structural components is paramount, transforming your manuscript from a collection of scenes into a cohesive, compelling narrative that haunts the reader well beyond the final page.

Chapter 2

Scene-Level Revisions

Diving into the microcosm of your horror narrative, scene-level revisions are where the visceral heartbeat of your story resides. Each scene, a cog in the machine, must not only function on its own with a clear purpose but also contribute to the larger narrative, character arcs, and the omnipresent cloak of horror that envelops your tale. This chapter explores the art of refining individual scenes, focusing on their purpose, the natural flow of dialogue, and the golden rule of "show, don't tell."

Scene Purpose and Impact

Every scene in your horror story should serve a purpose, whether advancing the plot, deepening character development, or enhancing the horror elements. A scene without a clear purpose risks diluting the tension and pacing, potentially disengaging your readers.

- Evaluate Purpose: Review each scene and ask, "What is the purpose of this scene?" If it doesn't clearly advance the story, reveal something new about a character, or heighten the horror atmosphere, consider revising or removing it.

- Assess Impact: Beyond its purpose, assess the scene's impact. Does a seemingly quiet moment between characters set the stage for a later revelation? Does an exploration of a dark corridor amplify the sense of dread? Ensure each scene contributes to building suspense and emotional investment.

Dialogue Refinement

Dialogue breathes life into your characters and can be a powerful tool in escalating horror. It should feel natural, reflect the character's background and current emotional state, and serve the scene's purpose.

- Character-Appropriate: Ensure the dialogue matches the character's voice. A teenager's speech will differ from an elderly occult expert's. Each character's background, education, and personality should inform how they speak.

- Serve the Story: Dialogue should always serve the story, whether revealing crucial plot points, showcasing character dynamics, or contributing to the atmosphere. Unnecessary banter can dilute the tension, so trim dialogue that doesn't serve a clear purpose.

- Horror Element: In horror, dialogue can also serve as a subtle tool for amplifying dread. An offhand remark about an urban legend, a whispered warning, or a broken, fearful confession can all elevate the scene's tension.

Show, Don't Tell

"Show, don't tell" is a foundational principle in writing, especially vital in horror, where the aim is to immerse readers in an experience that evokes fear and suspense.

- Visualize Actions and Emotions: Instead of stating a character is scared, describe their physical reactions—pale skin, trembling hands, a choked scream. This not only shows their fear but also makes it palpable to the reader.

- Use Sensory Details: Engage all senses to bring scenes to life. The musty smell of an old house, the eerie silence of a fog-laden forest, or the cold touch of an unseen presence can all "show" the horror more effectively than simply stating it.

- Reveal Through Actions: Characters' actions can reveal their personalities, fears, and motivations more effectively than exposition. Show a character's bravery through their decision to investigate a noise, or their denial of the supernatural through dismissive actions, rather than explanatory dialogue.

Scene-level revisions are where the precision of your craft comes into play, honing each scene to ensure it's a vital part of the story's body. By meticulously evaluating each scene's purpose and impact, refining dialogue for natural flow and character authenticity, and adhering to the "show, don't tell" principle, you elevate the narrative from a mere story to an immersive horror experience. Each scene becomes a step deeper into the dark, a moment that either tightens the tension or offers a fleeting respite, only to plunge the reader back into the abyss. In the tapestry of your horror tale, every scene, every line of dialogue, and every described detail is a thread woven with intention, crafting a narrative that ensnares and terrifies in equal measure.

Chapter 3
Fine-Tuning Prose

In the shadows of horror fiction, where every word can cast a spell of dread or illuminate a path to deeper understanding, fine-tuning your prose is akin to sharpening your most trusted blade. This chapter delves into refining your writing to achieve crystal-clear clarity, evoke vivid sensory experiences, and maintain a consistent voice and tone that resonates with the chilling essence of the genre.

Clarity and Conciseness

In the dance of horror storytelling, every step, every word, must be deliberate. Clarity and conciseness are your guides through the mist, ensuring that your narrative doesn't lose its way in the dark.

- Trim the Fat: Review your manuscript for redundancy, repetition, and fluff. Each word should serve a purpose, either advancing the plot, deepening character insight, or enhancing the atmosphere. If it doesn't, it's chaff to be cut.

- Simplify Complex Sentences: Long, convoluted sentences can confuse readers and dilute the impact of your scenes. Break them down, keep them direct. Let the complexity of your ideas, not your sentence structure, intrigue the reader.

- Active vs. Passive Voice: Active voice lends immediacy and impact, vital in horror where every moment counts. "The door slammed shut by an unseen force" becomes "An unseen force slammed the door shut," making the action more direct and forceful.

Sensory Details and Imagery

Horror thrives on the ability to transport readers into a world where the ordinary becomes terrifyingly extraordinary. Sensory details and vivid imagery are your portals to this realm.

- Engage All Senses: Go beyond sight and sound. The coppery taste of fear, the suffocating smell of decay, the icy touch of a ghostly presence—employ all senses to immerse the reader in the scene.

- Use Metaphors and Similes Wisely: Metaphors and similes can add depth and dimension to your descriptions but use them sparingly and thoughtfully. A well-placed metaphor can illuminate, while an ill-chosen one can obscure.

- Descriptive Precision: When describing horror elements, be precise yet evocative. The shape lurking in the shadows isn't just "dark"; it's "a patch of darkness where light fears to tread."

Voice and Tone Consistency

The voice and tone of your narrative are the soul of your horror story, setting the mood and guiding the reader's emotional journey.

- Establish a Strong Narrative Voice: Whether you're channeling an unreliable narrator or a detached omniscient entity, ensure the voice is compelling and distinct, capable of carrying the weight of the horror you wish to convey.

- Maintain Tone Consistency: The tone should reflect the genre and story. A Gothic horror will have a different tone from a psychological thriller. Be wary of tonal shifts that could jar the reader out of the story, unless deliberately used to enhance the narrative.

- Genre Appropriateness: Ensure your prose style and tone align with horror fiction conventions while still offering a fresh perspective. Avoid overly flowery language that might dilute the tension, opting instead for a style that amplifies the impending sense of doom.

Fine-tuning your prose is the meticulous process of ensuring that every word, every sentence, contributes to the overarching horror narrative. By striving for clarity and conciseness, you ensure that your story remains sharp and focused, a blade cutting through the darkness. With sensory details and imagery, you paint a world that's vividly terrifying, inviting readers to step inside and experience the horror firsthand. And through a consistent voice and tone, you weave a spell that holds them captive, suspended in the terror you've conjured. In the craft of horror writing, your prose is not just a means of telling a story; it's the very medium through which fear is born, nurtured, and unleashed upon the imagination.

Chapter 4

Horror-Specific Considerations

In the unique tapestry of horror fiction, where every shadow whispers secrets and every silence screams, certain considerations are pivotal in crafting a narrative that ensnares the mind and quickens the pulse. This chapter explores the nuanced aspects of revising horror stories, focusing on the meticulous construction of suspense, the delicate balance of horror and gore, and the interplay between psychological and physical horror.

Building and Sustaining Suspense

Suspense is the lifeblood of horror fiction, the slow drip that keeps readers on the edge of their seats, hearts racing in anticipation of the unknown.

- Pace with Purpose: Review your scenes for pacing, ensuring that the buildup of suspense is neither too rushed to be believed nor too slow to maintain tension. Use shorter scenes and sentences to quicken the pace and heighten suspense, and longer ones to build atmosphere and anticipation.

- Cliffhangers and Revelations: End scenes and chapters on notes that compel the reader to turn the page. Be it a startling revelation, a whispered threat, or an unanswered question, each should pull the reader deeper into the web of your story.

- Subvert Expectations: Play with readers' expectations by setting up familiar horror tropes only to twist them in unexpected ways. This not only refreshes classic horror elements but also keeps readers guessing, enhancing the suspense.

Managing Horror and Gore

The depiction of horror and gore must be handled with a keen sense of balance, ensuring that it serves the story and evokes the desired emotional response without numbing the reader to the terror.

- Serve the Story: Ensure that every instance of horror or gore advances the plot or deepens character development. Gratuitous violence that doesn't serve a purpose can desensitize readers and detract from the emotional impact.

- Imply More Than Show: Sometimes, the suggestion of horror is more potent than explicit description. The sound of dragging chains, the glimpse of a shadow, or the aftermath of violence can be more unsettling than a detailed account of the act itself.

- Know Your Audience: Consider the tolerance level of your intended audience for horror and gore. Tailoring the intensity of your scenes to your audience's expectations can enhance engagement without crossing the line into repulsion.

Psychological vs. Physical Horror

Horror fiction often treads the line between the terrors of the mind and those of the physical world. Striking the right balance between these elements is crucial for a narrative that resonates deeply with readers.

- Evaluate the Balance: Reflect on your story's reliance on psychological vs. physical horror. A tale rooted in the character's mental unraveling will have a different balance than one focused on tangible threats.

- Complement, Don't Compete: Ensure that psychological and physical horror elements complement each other rather than compete for attention. A physical threat can heighten the psychological tension, while the mental state of characters can amplify the fear of physical horrors.

- Use Psychological Depth to Enhance Fear: Deepen the psychological horror by exploring characters' fears, traumas, and vulnerabilities. This not only adds depth to your characters but also makes the physical horror more impactful, as readers understand and share the characters' dread.

Revising horror fiction demands a delicate touch, a keen awareness of the genre's unique requirements, and an understanding of how to weave suspense, horror, and character psychology into a tapestry that captivates and terrifies. By fine-tuning your narrative to build and sustain suspense, carefully managing the depiction of horror and gore, and thoughtfully balancing psychological and physical elements, you can craft a story that not only scares but also resonates with readers on a visceral level. In the shadowed corridors of horror fiction, these considerations are your guiding lanterns, illuminating the path to a tale that lingers in the mind long after the last page is turned.

Chapter 5

Grammar, Spelling, and Punctuation

In the meticulous craft of horror writing, where every word is a brushstroke on a canvas of dread, the importance of grammar, spelling, and punctuation cannot be overstated. These fundamental aspects of writing serve as the invisible threads that hold the fabric of your narrative together, ensuring clarity, coherence, and professionalism. This chapter delves into the crucial final steps of proofreading and formatting consistency, which, while seemingly mundane, are essential in polishing your manuscript to a gleaming edge.

Proofreading

The final barrier between your manuscript and its readers, proofreading is the meticulous process of scouring your text for the lurking errors that can disrupt the immersive experience of horror.

- Grammatical Precision: Grammar errors can jolt readers out of the story, breaking the spell of horror you've woven. Pay close attention to common issues like subject-verb agreement, correct tense usage, and proper sentence structure. Tools like grammar checkers can help, but a human touch is irreplaceable for catching the subtleties of language.

- Spelling Scrutiny: Spelling mistakes can undermine the credibility of your narrative and distract from the tension. Use spell checkers as a first line of defense but follow up with a careful manual review, especially for homophones (words that sound alike but have different meanings) and horror-specific terminology that might be unfamiliar or unique to your story.

- Punctuation Precision: Punctuation guides the rhythm of your prose, the ebb and flow of suspense and revelation. Ensure commas, periods, dashes, and ellipses are used correctly to convey the intended pacing and pauses. Misplaced punctuation can alter the meaning of a sentence or disrupt the flow, pulling readers out of the moment.

Formatting Consistency

The presentation of your manuscript, though less about the craft of writing, plays a significant role in reader perception and engagement. Consistent formatting ensures that nothing distracts from the chilling tale you've crafted.

- Chapter Headings: Maintain uniformity in chapter titles or headings in terms of font size, style, and placement, especially when using dates, times, and locations in your headings. This consistency helps readers navigate your story and maintains a professional appearance.

- Indents and Spacing: Standardize paragraph indents and line spacing throughout your manuscript. Inconsistent spacing can make your text appear disorganized and can be jarring for readers as they move through your story.

- Font Usage: Choose a clear, readable font and stick with it throughout the manuscript. The font size should also be consistent, with possible exceptions for chapter titles or specific stylistic choices, such as letters or diary entries within the narrative.

While the elements of grammar, spelling, punctuation, and formatting might seem peripheral compared to the crafting of suspenseful scenes and complex characters, they are the polish that makes your story shine in the dim light of a horror-filled room. Proofreading and consistent formatting are not merely about correctness. They are about respecting your readers and providing them with a seamless, immersive experience. As you venture into the final stages of preparing your horror manuscript, remember that these fundamental aspects of writing serve as the foundation upon which the terror of your narrative stands. A story free from the distractions of errors allows the true horror to unfold in the minds of your readers, unimpeded and unforgettable.

Chapter 6

Feedback and External Perspectives

In the solitary endeavor of horror writing, where authors conjure terrors from the depths of their imagination, the value of external perspectives cannot be understated. This chapter explores the crucial role of feedback in refining your horror narrative, from the insightful critiques of beta readers and partners to the specialized expertise of professional editors.

Beta Readers and Critique Partners

The first line of defense against narrative blind spots, beta readers, and critique partners offer invaluable insights that can illuminate overlooked strengths and weaknesses in your manuscript.

- Choosing Your Readers: Select beta readers and critique partners who understand the horror genre and, ideally, your specific sub-genre. Their familiarity with horror conventions can provide targeted feedback on how your story measures up to genre expectations and where it stands out.

- Interpreting Feedback: Receiving criticism can be daunting, but it's crucial for growth. Look for common themes in the feedback—if multiple readers point out the same issue, it's likely an area that needs work. However, also trust your instincts; not all advice will align with your vision for the story.

- Actionable Insights: Use the feedback to make actionable revisions. Specific comments on pacing, character development, or plot inconsistencies can guide your editing process, enhancing the overall impact of your horror narrative.

Professional Editing Services

While feedback from peers is invaluable, the expertise of a professional editor can elevate your manuscript to a professional standard, ensuring it's polished and ready for publication.

- Developmental Editing: This service focuses on the "big picture" elements of your manuscript, such as plot structure, character arcs, and thematic coherence. A developmental editor can help ensure your horror story is compelling, cohesive, and effectively paced.

- Line Editing: Line editors delve into the prose itself, refining sentence structure, dialogue, and narrative flow. Their focus is on enhancing clarity, style, and readability, ensuring each sentence contributes to building suspense and atmosphere.

- Copyediting: The copyeditor's realm is the technical aspects of writing—grammar, punctuation, spelling, and consistency. This meticulous review is essential for catching errors that could distract readers and detract from the immersive horror experience.

Embracing feedback and external perspectives is a testament to the dedication to your craft. Beta readers and critique partners provide the first layer of insight, highlighting areas for improvement and aspects of your story that resonate. Professional editors bring specialized skills to refine your narrative further, from overarching structural elements to the fine details of grammar and style. Together, these external perspectives are invaluable in transforming your manuscript from a rough gem to a polished work of horror that captivates and terrifies readers, leaving a lasting imprint in the shadowy corners of their minds.

Chapter 7

Revision Strategies and Practices

Navigating the labyrinth of revision in horror fiction is akin to threading through a haunted forest, where every path could lead to new discoveries or back to familiar haunts. This chapter outlines a strategic approach to the revision process, offering guidance on creating a plan, prioritizing edits, and confronting the specters of attachment, conflicting feedback, and the elusive sense of completion.

Revision Plan

A well-structured revision plan is your map through the thicket of changes, ensuring that your efforts are both efficient and effective.

- Sequential Approach: Consider tackling revisions in layers, starting with broad structural edits before moving to scene-level adjustments and finally honing in on line edits and prose refinement. This prevents the need for reworking the same sections multiple times due to overarching changes.

- Prioritize Edits: Begin with changes that have the most significant impact on your narrative. Addressing major plot holes or character inconsistencies early on can shape the direction of subsequent revisions.

- Organize the Process: Use tools like chapter outlines, revision check-lists, or software that allows for easy navigation and note-taking within your manuscript. Keeping your revisions organized can prevent over-whelm and ensure no aspect is overlooked.

Dealing with Common Challenges

The revision journey is fraught with challenges, from personal attachment to your writing to navigating the murky waters of feedback.

- Overcoming Attachment: Writers often feel a deep connection to their scenes, characters, or even specific lines. However, every element in the story must earn its place. If a scene doesn't serve the plot or enhance the horror atmosphere, it may need to be cut or revised, no matter how attached you are to it.

- Conflicting Feedback: Receiving divergent opinions from beta readers or editors can be confusing. Look for consensus where it exists, but also weigh feedback against your vision for the story. In the end, the story is yours, and revisions should align with your goals for the narrative.

- Knowing When It's "Done": One of the most daunting challenges is recognizing when to step back and declare the story complete. No work will ever be perfect, and part of the writer's journey is learning to accept this. If you've addressed the significant issues and further changes are no longer improving the story but merely altering it, it may be time to consider your story "done."

Revision is a crucial phase in the life cycle of your horror story, a time for reshaping and refining the raw material of your first draft into a polished and terrifying narrative. By approaching this phase with a structured plan, you can navigate the complexities of revision with purpose and clarity. Embrace the challenges as part of the creative process, recognizing that each hurdle overcome adds depth and strength to your story. With perseverance and strategic revision practices, you can transform the initial draft's raw terror into a refined nightmare that ensnares the imaginations of your readers, guiding them through a meticulously crafted landscape of fear.

The Final Journey

As the shadows lengthen and the echoes of your horror narrative begin to fade, you arrive at the final stage of your journey—the last read-through, the moment where your story undergoes its final transformation. This concluding phase is not merely about dotting the i's and crossing the t's; it's a ritual of refinement, a final incantation to summon the true essence of your tale from the depths of the written word.

The Last Read-Through

The last read-through is your final opportunity to ensure that your manuscript is as polished and potent as it can be, free from the earthly tethers of errors and inconsistencies that might diminish its power to haunt and horrify.

- Reading Aloud: There is magic in the spoken word, a power to evoke and ensnare. By reading your manuscript aloud, you can catch rhythm issues, awkward phrasings, and dialogue that doesn't ring true. The sound of your voice breathing life into the words can reveal much about the flow and impact of your narrative.

- Fresh Eyes: Familiarity breeds invisibility; the more you look at something, the less you see it. Altering the font, size, or format of your text can trick your brain into seeing your manuscript anew, allowing you to catch errors and inconsistencies that previously slipped through.

- The Clean Sweep: Ensure your manuscript is as clean as possible. Look for typos, grammatical errors, and formatting issues that could distract or detract from the reader's experience. This final sweep is not just about correctness; it's about crafting a seamless vessel for your story to inhabit.

Embarking on the Final Journey

As you stand at the threshold of completion, manuscript in hand, remember that the journey of horror writing is one of constant transformation. From the nascent seed of an idea to the sprawling labyrinth of revision, each step has shaped and honed your narrative into its final form. The last read-through, with its focus on clarity, rhythm, and polish, is the culmination of this process, the final turn of the key that unlocks the true potential of your story.

In the quiet moments of this last pass, as you whisper your words into the stillness and scrutinize each line for imperfection, know that you are not merely editing a document. You are imbuing your tale with the final touches of a craftsman, ensuring that when it ventures forth into the world, it carries with it the full weight of your intent and the depth of your creative spirit.

Let this conclusion not be an end but a gateway, a passage from the world of creation to the realm of sharing your nightmares and dreams with those who dare to delve into the darkness you've conjured. Your story, polished and perfected, is ready to stand as a testament to the journey you've undertaken, a beacon to guide others through the twisted landscapes of horror that you've so meticulously crafted.

Section 6

Writer's life

Chapter 1

Become Your Own Patron: Living the Dream, Funding the Reality - Brian Hodge

I used to never talk about this. Ever.

The self-imposed gag order was no doubt a carryover from the thoroughly American Midwest upbringing I had, which served me well in many respects...but also, at an early age, used a permanent marker to jot in my head a list of topics to be excluded from polite conversation.

Wherever you grew up, maybe you heard it yourself: *We don't talk about money.*

Why loosen the gag here? A few years back I was one of numerous authors involved with a publisher that had, for years, maintained an excellent reputation. Until it collapsed, seemingly overnight. It was like watching a dam burst. It was the bad-news equivalent of Shakespeare's line in *Hamlet*: "When sorrows come, they come not single spies, but in battalions."

The transgressions and malfeasances were many and varied, including financial.

As the shockwaves rippled, people who were owed royalties and advances—but had been holding out hope—began to confront the possibility of being stiffed on what was due them. Social media is made for such conversations. People feeling angry, feeling betrayed, can't type fast enough. It became obvious that some of the participants had been counting on this money. They needed it and they needed it yesterday.

Two predominant emotional reactions erupt during such situations. I felt one of them. People were understandably infuriated—no different here, under this roof.

What I didn't feel was panic.

To be sure, I love getting paid. Paper checks, bank transfers, those three sweet words from PayPal: *You've got money.*

But I've also spent the last twenty-six years striving to build a financial bulwark against the kind of lamentable news cited above, so that however infuriating it may be, it is denied the power to hurt me.

For those folks who were plainly hurt by the news and bracing for pain in their everyday lives, I felt bad. I knew exactly what it felt like, because I've been there, too—you'll see. In this situation's drawn-out aftermath, it began to weigh on me: Maybe there should be more conversations about money.

Silence on a topic, combined with the scattered isolation of its affected human constituents, is how malefactors and existential asteroid strikes get the better of us.

Pop Quiz, Part 1

Here are a couple of questions worth taking some time to ponder.

First: What is money to you? Beyond the Economics 101 definitions, I mean. The key words here are *to you.*

The world is full of people for whom money is, first and foremost, a way of keeping score. Their main metric for measuring themselves against the next person; against people they've never met. The trap here is that there's always a higher score to rack up and no buzzer to signal the end of the game, other than the flatline tone of a cardiac monitor.

A friend of mine works a well-paid part-time job as personal assistant to a man worth, last I heard, around ten million dollars. He's sufficiently up in years that it's hard to imagine him spending it all. Yet, according to my friend, he lives in fear of losing it. He lives in continual dread of *less*.

That's a scorekeeper.

Then there are those of us—count me among them—whose regard for money comes from its potential to provide the foundations of a satisfying life. Money means options. Freedom. Choices. Autonomy.

Yes, you could apply perceptions of lack here, too. There's always going to be a greater range of choices to be enjoyed, and higher levels of autonomy. But it still seems the healthier mindset, because it remains focused on possibilities.

Pop Quiz, Part 2

Next question: What do you want? What do you cherish? What do you *value*?

A surprising number of people are more in touch with what they don't want. But if you're reading a book like this, you're likely clear on at least one thing: You want to write, and you're serious about that.

In recent years I've taken to leading off my bio paragraphs for anthology appearances, etc., with a line describing myself as one of those people who always has to be making something.

Making stuff has been the prime mover for nearly my entire life ... a life that I have, as much as I could, arranged around and aligned with that pursuit. Not just writing, but music, photography, and whatever else comes to mind on occasion.

Making stuff, and the time and freedom to keep doing it, are what I have valued above pretty much all else...at times, more than security; more than the good opinions of my parents; even, a time or three, more than my mental and emotional health.

Once you identify what you want, what you *really* want, the question expands: How bad do you want it? What are you willing to do, to sacrifice, to obtain or achieve it? What is an acceptable price?

I've seen this credited as a Spanish proverb, a Persian proverb, and a stark variant of the story of Adam and Eve first getting their marching orders in the Garden of Eden: *Take what you want, God said, and pay for it.*

Everything that follows from here should make the most sense when seen in that context: figuring out ways to pay for the life you want.

Bad News, Worse News

For the artist of whatever stripe—writer, musician, visual artist, performer—it is the dream: to devote yourself to your calling on a full-time basis, to cultivate an audience for it, to make it your life and livelihood, and live that life as authentically as possible.

But the dream is a nearsighted possum on the road, while Life, in the broader sense, is an 18-wheeler that isn't going to swerve.

It gets worse. It's common to embark upon this journey dreaming of hitting an early grand slam home run, so your career is locked in for the foreseeable future and you're financially set for life.

Few ever ride that catapult, even if they do the work and find an audience. The career and financial reality, for most of us, is a long, slow, tortuous grind, figuring things out along the way, course-correcting as needed, and, perhaps, redefining what fulfillment looks like.

If it's any consolation, the grand slam isn't an automatic guaranteed good thing. Rosters of lottery winners are replete with people who ended up broke, and in worse shape than they were before. Usually because, lacking the financial mindset to handle it, they weren't ready for it.

In Praise of Unreason

As has been pointed out by generations of sensible people, regardless of your talent and efforts, it's incredibly difficult to monetize your craft enough to keep you in food, clothing, shelter, and your favorite vices on an ongoing basis.

As the world's most annoying maxim goes: If it was easy, everybody would be doing it.

Staring down the blood-spattered grill of that 18-wheeler is enough to deter a lot of people. And, if there's something beautiful and wondrous inside them that still insists on having its say, steer them onto the middle path advocated by sensible folk: *Find your passion, then follow it on nights and weekends for the rest of your life.*

Entirely understandable and honorable. Live some form of the dream to whatever extent you can squeeze in during your off-hours.

But if that's still not good enough for you? If you still want to roll the bones and refuse to let sensible people have the last prudent word? Then we sound like kindred souls, you and I. You, me, and George Bernard Shaw:

"The reasonable man adapts himself to the world; the unreasonable man persists in trying to adapt the world to himself. Therefore all progress depends on the unreasonable man."

I have devoted my entire adult life—have expended blood and treasure, sweat and toil and tears—to adapting the world to myself. Not the whole world, certainly, but my patch of mountainous turf upon it.

For the unreasonable maker-of-stuff, there is no one-size-fits-all approach to becoming your own patron and funding the dream. Life circumstances, resources, temperaments, opportunities, inclinations, and a long list of other factors are as individualized as fingerprints and retinal scans.

To cut to the chase, the topic I never talked about: I accomplished this through investing in the stock market. Taking money that I made from writing and putting it to work, and continuing to add to it.

This is something I neither encourage nor discourage in anyone else. Nobody else can tell you what, exactly, to do to give yourself the best shot at staking out the life you'd like to live, and paying for it. Anybody who advises you to do *exactly* what they did probably has something to sell you, or a social media channel they want you to subscribe to.

At best, all I can do is tell you what I did, and why, in hopes that you can take a few useful bits; that something here will inspire you to find your own sustainable path in service to your creative vision.

So think principles here, rather than specifics. In the same way you wouldn't plagiarize someone else's work, but instead tap into the spirit behind it, use whatever lights you up as inspiration to create your own riff on the theme.

Maybe you want to live the dream full-time. Or maybe you'd be happy with the freedom to reduce your hours working for someone else's vision so you can devote them to your own. Ultimately, paying for this demands charting a course that's right for you, whatever it might look like: Any of a jillion side hustles. Developing and coding apps to sell. Launching and monetizing a YouTube channel. Setting your own hours driving as a medical courier. Drop-shipping via Amazon. Flipping fixer-upper houses. Or, so be it, investing.

Caveat #1: A personal disclaimer. While I'll be getting into actions I took and decisions I made, none of this was done in a vacuum of solitude. My lifelong love Doli was there through all of it. I couldn't have genetically engineered a more supportive, more encouraging, partner, and I strive to be the same for her. We have each other's backs, and she's had mine at some crucial times.

Caveat #2: Nothing is for everybody; no exception here. I know of no way of living one's life on one's own terms, and not being a pauper in the process, that doesn't demand certain qualities that are non-negotiables: Discipline. Long-term vision and longer-term patience. An ass that holds up to being repeatedly worked off. Tolerance for calculated risk. A level of stubbornness that makes mules look agreeable.

If you're all about immediate gratification...if you want the world and you want it now ... if you have trouble following through with commitments...then best of luck to you, and *vaya con Dios*. I can offer nothing here that aligns with that perspective.

This is playing life on offense. When it comes to money, and its role in your dreams and future, a strategy of sitting back and hoping for the best, that things will just work out, is...ehh, kind of like hoping that dose of flesh-eating bacteria will clear up on its own.

I've tried that, too. It doesn't work for long. Offense is better.

Fanaticism for Fun, Profit, and Soul-Crushing Disappointment

A necessary selection of autobiographical highlights:

My love of books and writing began before I even knew the alphabet. After spending my high school and college years winning and placing in various writing competitions, I got serious about it straight out of university. Academically, I'd made other plans, but *this* was what I yearned to do. Within a few years, my first two novels sold, three months apart, to New York publishers.

So I quit my full-time office job and, for three years, worked a part-time late-night gig as the janitor for an upscale auto dealership, to give myself more prime writing time while weaning myself off regular paychecks. After I became one of the first authors signed for the renowned Dell Abyss line of books, I emptied the mop bucket for the last time and have never clocked in for an outside job since.

My aim, from the beginning, was to do this full-time as soon as possible, and if I couldn't make that work, then I saw no point in existing. A writer was what I was, and I wouldn't *want* to exist any other way. This strikes me as a ridiculously hardline outlook now, but I was deadly serious about it at the time, and at least this fanatical self-assessment kept an eternal flame lit under me.

And I made it work. For a few years, anyway—good years, to be sure—but after the Dell Abyss line faded away, the sustainability of my path started to look rockier and rockier.

While I worked on the next novel, number seven, there was a relatively brief stint doing some scripting for a muscled-up metal singer who had launched his own comics company. For this I was eventually paid a $4600 rubber check. Not because the money wasn't there, but because this entrepreneurial, errm, *misfit* emptied the account the checks were drawn against. According to the appalled managing editor, this was to teach a lesson to everyone who'd spent the past few months asking about being paid for their work. Like, y'know, the contracts said. The lesson? *That we needed him.*

So yes...I know well the woes of assholes, egos, gross mismanagement, and unbridled fuckery body-slamming you at the worst possible time.

On the other hand, it's amusing to now look back on this era, and imagine a council of Greek gods and Muses gazing down and nodding to one another with approval. Because, if there's one thing they appreciate, it's the relentless struggles of a stalwart and expressive heart, be it engaged in warfare or art.

Look, he's still at it. Maybe he's suffered enough for now, Melpomene says to the others. *How about we let him have this next one?*

Out of the Mouths of Glue-Sniffers

That seventh novel? After it went nowhere with the literary agent I was trying out at the time—my fourth—I tightened the manuscript by 10%, gave it a new title, and changed agents yet again. The new one took it to auction, with four New York publishing houses bidding on it. William Morrow won out, buying it as one of their twelve lead titles for the next year.

I wish I could say this was only the first time that happened. But, so far, it hasn't again.

I wish I could say this was the beginning of a long, fruitful relationship with Morrow. But it wasn't. By the time my follow-up novel was done, Morrow had been bought and taken over by an even larger media conglomerate. Everyone I'd worked with had been jettisoned in three waves of mass firings. The incoming new regime had their own plans, and pretty much all the extant Morrow authors got the boot.

A crushing development, that. Even so, one titanic blessing had already been bestowed.

Publication, for an aspiring author, is a life-changing event. It shows you what's possible, what you're capable of. It provides you with a rung from which you can continue to climb. In a world of people who merely talk, you have DONE.

Having a book sell at auction is an even more epochal life-changing event. The variable here is, what do we mean by *life*? Short-term? You deposit your checks, hop on the hedonic treadmill, and once you've burned through the bucks it's back to the way things were before?

Or are we talking about enacting some changes that will echo for a lifetime?

And now, finally, we're really getting to it here.

Around that time I had the great fortune of learning that Joey Ramone, the since-deceased frontman of the proto-punk band the Ramones, was an avid investor. And good at it.

Wait. Joey Ramone, really? The tall, gawky-looking, fishbelly-pale guy in the leather jacket and jeans who sings lines like "I wanna be sedated," "beat on the brat," and "now I wanna sniff some glue"—*that* Joey Ramone?

The same. The kill shot from this discovery was his remark that he'd made way more money from investing than he ever had from music.

Not that I'd pondered it, but to this point I would've thought, perhaps naively, that he was rolling in it from what looked like a successful music career.

I'd been hearing the Ramones since I was a teenager. They were the focus of a cult movie. They did the theme song to the first film adaptation of Stephen King's *Pet Sematary*. Joey Ramone was a familiar face on MTV, and acted as studio producer for other artists.

Yet here he was saying that the bulk of his livelihood had come, not from what the world knew him for, but from something that appeared comically incongruent with his image.

The implied corollary was that it was the investing that had enabled him to keep making music on his own terms, and thus live the artist's life that he wanted to.

Of all the things I've blundered across in my life, few have been better timed than this.

Pay attention to the synchronicities in your life. It may be the universe trying to tell you something.

Taking the Hint

So that's when and why I became an investor. I opened an account at Fidelity and started putting part of the proceeds from this auctioned novel to work. There might never be a better chance; might never be another chance like this at all.

Twenty-six years later, I can state that the difference it has made in being an inveterate maker of stuff is incalculable.

Crucially, it wasn't a one-time outlay. Within a couple of years, I embarked upon a side hustle: freelancing for a publishing group that put out several monthly magazines on computers, consumer electronics, and a trade journal for IT professionals. Result: a decade of multiple articles each month, at 40 cents/word, for living expenses and to continue to feed the portfolio.

Sometimes, if you look beneath the surface of something you're doing already, you can spot further opportunities to take advantage of. After developing friendly contacts in the PR and marketing departments of various consumer electronics manufacturers, I discovered that from some of them I could buy items for what was called "media price"—wholesale, roughly. No rule said I had to keep them. So, instead, I would flip them on eBay for a profit, and the happy buyer still got a bargain.

Hustle, grind, put the proceeds to work, repeat. All in the service of the greater vision: maximizing the freedom to live as someone who always has to be making something, but *without* having to depend on the success of any one project, or risk being left devastated by its failure.

Tending this portfolio of stocks, mutual funds, index funds, and ETFs has necessitated a course of self-study that continues to this day. Which has included, either on an ongoing basis or along the way:

- Building a library of dozens of books on money, personal finance, and investing.

- Subscribing to a third-party newsletter specifically for investors at Fidelity.

- Hiring a fiduciary advisor for counsel and oversight.

- Periodically rebalancing accounts to realign them with the targeted asset allocation that the advisor and I have come up with.

- Exercising the essential quality of patience.

Time is the greatest ally here. Here's what time brings: Interest. Dividends. Capital gains distributions. Asset appreciation. It all counts; all adds up over time. They're there if you need them, and on many occasions I did, and was glad they were, because that's what they were there *for*.

Still, the paradoxical trick is to *not* need them for as long as you can. When interest, dividends, and distributions are automatically reinvested, instead of being withdrawn, for year upon year, then you get what has been described as one of the most powerful forces in the universe: compounding. A snowball effect when your earnings start to earn, and *those* earnings earn, and so on.

The Compound Benefits of Having Your Shit Together

Coming up on six years ago, as I write this, I lost both parents three weeks apart. Neither death was expected, dual blows exacerbated by the fact that when the court appoints you as estate executor, you're expected to hit the ground running with your new legal responsibilities.

Sorting out the messes consumed the next year of my life, and much of it was new to me, with lots of learning on the job. Aided by the experience gained over the previous twenty years, I was able to meet every obligation and satisfy every legality.

More pertinent to our topic here, I was able to take over my parents' retirement accounts, managing them in place and keeping them growing, until I was legally in the clear to bring them over into my own portfolio without otherwise touching them, because I didn't need to.

Most crucially, I was able to do this without making any of the mistakes that can result in costly penalties to the unwary and the over-eager. There are no do-overs with some of this stuff. Screw it up, and what's lost is gone for good.

The moral of this sidebar story: Learning how to effectively save, invest, and manage money is a skill set—and a mindset—that will serve you and your people for a lifetime. Giving yourself the experience of diligently handling small amounts so you can better handle larger ones pays dividends of its own. This is vital at times of crisis and tragedy, if only because you're better equipped to keep a level head while all those about you are losing theirs.

Where to begin, if you've only been winging it until now? One may be out there, but I can't think of a better, more comprehensive single-stop beginner-friendly overview than the book *Money: Master the Game*, by Tony Robbins.

If that's too boomer for you, Ramit Sethi and his first book, *I Will Teach You to Be Rich*, has legions of fans who credit it with getting them started in the right direction and developing lasting good habits.

Spreading It Around

After those broad strokes, let's get more granular.

When you first began earning money—say, from your first job as a teenager—maybe that was when you opened your first bank account. A checking account, perhaps a savings account alongside it. Maybe things stayed this way for years. Maybe they're still that way.

There's something comforting about this kind of consolidation. It's simple. Straightforward. You review your monthly statement and immediately know where things stand. *Look at it. There it is. There's my money. Look at it just...sit there.*

Getting past this early mindset was one of the biggest hurdles I had to clear. I'm not sure what was behind it, but suspect it's not uncommon. Maybe it's because, when you start dividing up your lump—some going here, some going there—each sub-lump looks smaller. Maybe it's a control issue, born of a fear of not being able to keep watch on it to the same degree. Maybe having multiple accounts instead of one lies outside the comfort zone.

Attitudes toward money can be deeply irrational, and as tough to root out as any phobia.

After getting past this, I began a more systematic approach utilizing multiple accounts. Sometimes you'll see these referred to as buckets, with each bucket having its own job to do.

What the system currently looks like:

- A checking account with a local bank, that's mainly a hub for deposits, ATM access, debit card use, and paying bills.

- Three high-yield savings accounts with Goldman Sachs, accessed online. GS has been around since 1869, so I trust they're not going anywhere in my lifetime. The primary account is for general liquid cash, and also functions as a reserve in case of emergency.

- A second Goldman Sachs account for setting aside quarterly tax estimates. Once the money goes in I regard it as having entered a gulag, where it's still technically working, but otherwise given up for dead.

- A third GS account for saving for guilt-free dream expenditures. Think non-essential but larger-ticket things. Travel, for instance. The meandering trip around Iceland's Ring Road I want to take someday? It's in there.

- Those aforementioned accounts at Fidelity Investments: brokerage account, Roth IRA, the two IRAs taken over from my parents. The boring stuff. It's virtually all in a diversified selection of index funds now, split 62% in stocks and 38% in bonds.

- A couple relatively miniscule accounts at Wealthfront and M1 Finance, for more experimental plays. The fun stuff.

Accounts are linked as necessary, so it's quick and simple to transfer money wherever it needs to go. Including to the IRS, to directly give it its due.

How does this system work, in practice?

Let's say $100 comes in for dividing up and routing. The percentages become obvious that way.

- $20 to tax estimates. Dead to me, remember.

- $10 to long-term primary savings.

- $5 or $10 to dream savings.

- $10 or $15 to investing.

- Remainder hangs around for living expenses.

Am I rigorous about adhering to this breakdown? Hardly. It's just a guideline. I'm not drawing a predictable salary that this can be applied to with consistency. So it fluctuates according to variables like amounts and current balances.

What's most important is maintaining the underlying principle: Each of these buckets gets *something*, for its own job.

Let's Get Back to Your Art

Because your art is what this is all about, right?

Let's say you've been making stuff awhile. If you haven't, that's fine, because as long as you don't quit, someday you *will* have been at it awhile.

This brings up another point of inquiry worth exploring: How do you view your work? Your *body of work*, as it builds up over time?

Ideally, each individual work is conceived as a love child. You have this idea, it starts to grow, you surround it with characters you want to spend a lot of time around, and you commit to developing it until you've created this fully formed entity that would never have existed without your devotion and drive.

A labor of love. And the next. And the next. As a family, it can get quite extended. Each labor of love can help financially subsidize the begetting of *more* labors of love.

211

To date, mine consists of 13 published novels, with another big one in the works; 6 collections of short fiction, with the newest awaiting release; an omnibus edition; and closing on 140 shorter works ranging from a few hundred words to nearly 35,000.

Labors of love, one and all. Sometimes the love gets strained—at times to the point we start throwing things at each other—but it remains strong enough to keep us together.

Even so, I believe there's room for another, concurrent, way of looking at one's collective works. After decades of growing it, I experienced a change in thinking that was less a shift than an expansion, and a beneficial one, at that. Because how you look at an entity determines how you treat it, and how it treats you.

The love hadn't gone anywhere. At the same time, I began to regard these works as...well, as what they actually were all along: a body of intellectual property. It will never get any smaller; it should only continue to grow. Unlike technologies that become superseded by later technologies, it has no built-in obsolescence. And, with a handful of exceptions, such as the Hellboy projects I worked on—getting invited to play in someone else's yard, is how I think of those—it's all 100% mine.

Best practices, then, to keep the body healthy: Keep ownership and control in your favor for as much and as long as you can. Never turn these over to someone else in perpetuity. And never cut someone else in on rights that have nothing to do with publication, such as film rights.

For something like a short story or novella, it's reasonable to grant a publisher of your work a period of exclusivity. But the publishing rights should automatically revert to you after, at most, a year or two. So read that contract! Most details are negotiable. If you see something—rights, or a split of earnings percentages—that seems too skewed in the publisher's favor, at your expense, ask to change it. Ask nicely.

For books, contractual terms can be more varied and nuanced. Confusing, too. Periods of exclusivity can be much longer, after which rights may revert to you automatically. Or the publisher may retain the rights as long as the book is in print. And be advised, an e-book edition is a no-overhead way for a publisher to claim they're keeping your book in print. Sometimes after a book goes out of print, even though it's dormant, the publisher will retain the rights to it by default...*unless and until* you issue a formal written request for them to print a new edition; if they don't, only then will the rights revert to you.

So, again, read those contracts. Scrutinize the terms.

Why guard the ownership and control of your intellectual property like a grizzly bear minds her cubs?

Because your body of work is every bit a portfolio of assets as those you could buy shares in, except these are assets you've made yourself. They have the potential to keep working for you for years, decades, a lifetime.

In recent years, my work has generated income down a variety of avenues.

- Advance and/or delivery payments for new work.

- Royalties for print editions and e-books.

- Royalties for audiobooks.

- Reprint rights.

- Foreign translations and editions.

- Options for film and TV rights.

- Direct sales to readers.

The bigger your body of work, the greater the odds of individual works returning the favor and working for you. You never know what's going to step up and start earning again, perhaps long after you created it. Decades, even. Within the last couple of years, two of my earliest novels were optioned for TV under a production company's development deal with NBC Universal's Peacock.

Likewise, you never know what may strike a chord right away and start punching above its apparent weight. One particular novella of mine—maybe three weeks' work—due to its initial printing and later reprints and years of TV options, has not only brought in far more than any other piece of short fiction I've done. It's brought in more than a lot of authors see for entire novels.

You never know.

I couldn't have planned for either of these; couldn't have repeated them if I'd tried. They simply came about as a consequence of doing the work, doing the best work I was capable of doing at any given time, then moving on to do more work to keep growing the *body* of work.

Developments like these … they come, or they don't. It's better when they do. Obviously. Even when they do, however, they're erratic about it. So I don't count on them, because I can't. But I've made sure I don't have to. And that began with leveraging the positive developments that did.

Bracing for Blowback

I can hear the raised voices now. The objections. What author Steven Pressfield, in *The War of Art*, calls The Resistance. It's often an involuntary reaction, as quick as the twitch after the doctor's rubber mallet bonks your knee.

"Well, that's fine for *you*. What about those of us who *haven't* had a novel sell at auction? Who can't find a good side hustle? Who don't have as big a body of work? Who haven't gotten an agent? Who don't have the stomach for the ups and downs of the stock market? Or a supportive partner to share our dreams?"

The litany could go on awhile.

I get it. I understand, and empathize. I began with none of those things. Still, I didn't begin empty-handed. Two advantages were there from the start:

(1) I seem to have had an inborn base level of talent and inclination for writing, with an unflagging desire to get better at it, and found all this intrinsically rewarding.

(2) I had what I recognize now was one of the greatest intangible assets I could ever have asked for: the example of a father—a history teacher and coach turned school administrator—who managed his salary with great care and consideration.

So, yes, I fully recognize that environment matters. Background matters. What you absorb while growing up matters.

But the presence, or lack, of any particular attribute or advantage has never been the point here, any more than this has been about recommending someone follow a specific path.

No two paths are ever going to be the same. They can't be. Each person's path is the result of hundreds of thousands of wants and needs and decisions and impulses and unforeseen circumstances and opportunities and setbacks and random events and luck and life-currents too subtle to even perceive. Not even twins end up in the same place.

Rather, the only thing this can be about is:

Starting where you are, setting your intentions, working with what you have, and striving to make the most of what develops. Learning what you need to learn as it comes up. Recalibrating along the way. Getting knocked down, getting back up again. Wanting to quit, wanting to die, coming up with the reasons to keep going. Making bad decisions and learning from the consequences in order to make better ones.

Taking what you want, and paying for it...with the understanding that payment will take many forms.

Like Emily Dickinson, we dwell in Possibility.

I believed in the possibility of living life full-time as someone who makes stuff, and believed it was possible more fervently than any number of naysayers and reasonable people believed it wasn't.

That, if you can cultivate it, is a superpower.

Coda: 10 Principles for Fun, Profit, and Getting Through Soul-Crushing Disappointment

Whether we realize it, we all operate according to principles that guide our actions and decisions and daily habits. These have served me well, and had an immense positive impact on my mission to live as someone who always has to be making something.

Some pertain to doing the work. Some pertain to money. Some, to life overall.

None were in place from the start. Instead, they accrued over time, like an operating system getting upgraded with progressively better code. Some settled into place as soon as I was exposed to them. Others gelled as a result of recognizing some personal deficiency or fuck-up and thinking there had to be a better way.

Most I have violated or lost sight of, more than once, and when I have, it's nearly always been to my detriment. But, like lines of solid system code, they remain after the virus has been eradicated.

1. "Pay yourself first." If there's a universal maxim espoused by every financial advisor and money pundit, this is it. It goes back to those monetary buckets mentioned earlier, and pouring something into them right after income arrives. As the pundits usually elaborate, if you wait until the end of the month to save whatever's left over from what you've spent, it's amazing how little is left.

2. Live within your means. Better yet, live below them.

3. "The first hour is the rudder of the day."—Henry Ward Beecher

4. Breaking a promise or failing a commitment to someone else is shameful. Breaking promises or failing commitments I've made to myself, if I let it go on long enough, is crippling.

5. I can make progress, or I can make excuses, but not both.

6. Contractual agreements aside, nobody owes me anything. As Krishna tells Arjuna in the *Bhagavad Gita*, I have the right to my labor, but not to any particular fruits of my labor.

7. Rule #3 from *Road House*: "Be nice. Until it's time to not be nice."

8. Whatever I focus on, for good or for ill, tends to expand.

9. It doesn't matter who doesn't get it, doesn't get you, doesn't get what you do. What matters is who does. Focus on what matters.

10. "Absorb what is useful. Discard what is not. Add what is uniquely your own."—Bruce Lee

Chapter 2

Leveraging Technology in Writing

In the ever-evolving landscape of horror fiction, where the ancient dance of storytelling meets the cutting-edge of innovation, technology has become an indispensable ally to the modern writer. This chapter delves into the burgeoning world of emerging technologies—AI writing tools, virtual reality (VR), and interactive storytelling platforms—and how they can be harnessed to amplify the writing process and transform storytelling techniques.

AI Writing Tools: The Ghost in the Machine

Artificial intelligence has made significant inroads into the creative realm, offering tools that can assist writers in various aspects of the writing process, from generating ideas to refining prose.

- Idea Generation: AI tools can provide creative prompts, plot suggestions, and even character sketches, serving as a digital muse for writers seeking inspiration.

- Editing and Refinement: AI-powered editing software can go beyond basic grammar and spelling checks, offering suggestions for stylistic improvements, consistency, and even narrative flow, acting as a first line of defense in the editing process.

- Customization and Learning: Many AI tools have the capability to learn from user input, becoming more tailored to the writer's style and preferences over time, thereby becoming more of a personalized assistant than a generic tool.

Virtual Reality

Virtual reality technology offers a revolutionary way to experience and craft narratives, providing a fully immersive environment that can bring horror stories to life in unprecedented ways.

- World-Building: VR can be used by writers to "step into" their settings, exploring the worlds they create in a tangible way, which can deepen the descriptive process and ensure consistency in spatial and environmental details.

- Character Interaction: By interacting with characters within a VR environment, writers can gain new insights into character dynamics, spatial movement, and dialogue, enhancing the authenticity of interactions in their narratives.

- Reader Experience: Beyond the writing process, VR presents a novel medium for storytelling, allowing readers to experience horror narratives in an immersive, interactive format that could redefine the genre.

Interactive Storytelling Platforms

Interactive storytelling platforms represent the confluence of narrative and technology, where stories become not just tales to be told but worlds to be explored by the reader.

- Branching Narratives: These platforms allow for the creation of branching storylines, where readers make choices that affect the outcome of the story. This can be particularly compelling in horror fiction, where the stakes of decisions are high, and the tension is palpable.

- Engagement and Analytics: Interactive platforms offer the ability to track reader choices and engagement, providing valuable insights into reader preferences and behaviors, which can inform future storytelling strategies.

- Community Building: Many interactive storytelling platforms also foster communities of readers and writers, offering opportunities for feedback, collaboration, and shared storytelling experiences, enriching the creative process.

The integration of technology into the writing process represents a frontier of endless possibilities for horror writers. AI writing tools offer assistance and insights that can refine and enhance the writing process, while virtual reality technology provides a medium for unprecedented immersive world-building and character development. Interactive storytelling platforms, on the other hand, open up new avenues for narrative structure and reader engagement, transforming passive readers into active participants in the horror narrative. As writers harness these technologies, they not only streamline and enrich their creative process but also expand the very boundaries of horror storytelling, inviting readers into a world where the terror is as real as it is imagined. In this digital age, technology becomes the pen, the paper, and the path to uncharted realms of fear and fascination.

The Pros and Cons of AI for Authors

Before we look into the pros and cons of AI for authors, let's get something out of the way first. AI cannot and should not completely replace authors. AI is merely another tool that can make life easier for us. It's about ethical use. It's not nearly as human and creative as we are, and will hopefully never be.

So, let's explore this topic of growing relevance in the writing community. As AI technologies like ChatGPT become more integrated into our writing processes, it's vital to understand both its advantages and limitations. This piece aims to provide a balanced view, helping you make an informed decision about incorporating AI into your creative workflow.

Cons:

- Copyright issues: Content created with AI, like ChatGPT, isn't copyrightable. If you input your entire book, you can't claim copyright over the output. You also lose the ability to copyright whatever you put in. It's crucial to use AI-generated content as a starting point or in moments when you get stuck, and then infuse your own creativity and writing style.

- Beware of AI tech being used during Zoom or any other video-based meetings. This is mostly for companies, but everything said during those meetings becomes part of the AI world, and you won't be able to copyright it. So any new ideas or company secrets shared during those sessions are now basically public domain.

- There is of course the potential for errors. AI is still learning, and some of its sources definitely aren't reputable, so if you're writing non-fiction, be sure to double-check any facts or dates.

It's still relatively early days for using AI in your writing, so be prepared to be judged by your peers for being lazy.

An emerging consideration for authors using AI is the inclusion of AI clauses in publishing contracts. Publishers are increasingly adding these clauses, addressing the extent of AI involvement in manuscript creation. Authors who have relied significantly on AI for their work may face contractual limitations or challenges with certain publishers. It's crucial to carefully review contracts for AI-related stipulations to ensure compliance and understand how your use of AI in writing might impact publishing opportunities. If you merely use AI for ideas and brainstorming and keep it from writing the actual words in the manuscript, then you don't need to disclose using AI at all, since the written words are still yours.

Pros:

- The role of AI as a smart assistant for authors is multifaceted. It can answer questions, provide information, and offer guidance on various aspects of writing and publishing. Whether you need quick research, language suggestions, or insights into writing mechanics, AI can assist efficiently, enhancing productivity. It's like Google, but it feels more like having an actual conversation with a smart assistant who's there to help you.

- AI significantly saves time for authors in various ways. It streamlines research, quickly providing relevant information and references. For plotting and character development, AI can offer instant ideas and scenarios. This efficiency allows authors to focus more on refining their narratives and engaging creatively with their work, thus enhancing overall productivity in the writing process.

- AI is an invaluable tool for idea generation, particularly useful in brainstorming sessions and overcoming writer's block. It can suggest diverse storylines, character traits, and plot twists, providing fresh perspectives and creative stimuli. Authors can use AI to explore different narrative possibilities, experiment with genre blends, or refine story elements. This can invigorate the creative process, sparking new ideas or providing the impetus needed to move past creative hurdles.

- AI's role in content creation is a game-changer for authors. It can help craft engaging blog posts, social media updates, and even assist in drafting compelling synopses or book descriptions. This tool can provide initial drafts or ideas that authors can then refine and personalize. By handling the groundwork of content creation, AI allows authors to maintain a consistent online presence and marketing strategy, saving time and energy for their primary writing projects. Using a blog post as an example, you can write the initial, shortened blog post yourself, then ask ChatGPT to rewrite and expand. It's still your idea and your voice, but you had an assistant build on it.

Authors need to see AI as a supportive tool, enhancing your writing process without replacing your unique voice and creativity. While you may be hesitant, integrating AI thoughtfully can prevent falling behind in a tech-forward industry. Just be sure to always protect your copyright. Look into 'ChatGPT Enterprise' if you want to ensure you maintain copyright over everything you put into ChatGPT. But there's quite a waiting list.

*"Establishing a routine is easier said than done, especially when you're juggling multiple roles or titles in your life. Something I've very quickly had to learn after the birth of my daughter was to be gentle with myself. Some days I don't make it to the page and it's easy to get in my head about that, but my mental, physical, and emotional wellbeing always need to come first, and if I'm burning myself out, I'm of no use to anyone. So what does that look like for me now? I wake up at 4:30 a.m. a few times a week for some quiet writing time while everyone in my house is asleep (puppies included!). I take my vitamins, my medication, drink lots of water, and try to include some type of movement into my day. Sometimes this is yoga for my arms, neck, and back, and sometimes it's a quick walk at lunchtime. I make therapy a priority and I carry my notebook around with me to scribble poetry or daydreams down when I'm standing in line at the post office or in between teaching classes, and every day, no matter what is on my schedule, I always, always, **always** carve out time to read."*—**Stephanie M. Wytovich**

Chapter 3

Book Launches Part 2

Advanced Engagement and Community Building

Building a loyal readership involves more than just announcing new releases. It requires creating a sense of community and ongoing engagement with your audience over a long time. To what end, you might ask? To build trust mainly, and then to create interest and buzz. These days, we authors need to constantly post teasers and reminders that we exist, just like you'd see for a big movie release months before it's available; you'll get constant reminders, trailers, teasers, updates, and be a part of conversations with friends or online acquaintances (especially if it's a remake). That's what we need to aim for with books, as well. It's a long process that you need to dedicate time to though, at least 30 minutes a day. Perhaps an hour a day over weekends. Most of what makes a book launch successful are your pre-launch activities. What makes it successful after that will depend on the quality of your work and how much word-of-mouth it can generate. So you need to be active on social media, your newsletter, and interest groups. Go on podcasts and interviews, keep building your mailing list, and be active in your writing community. Help others. Contribute.

Physical Launch Events

Reach out to your local bookstores and writing groups. Take part in other people's launches so that you can both learn and network. Build up relationships and contacts with local journalists. Attend as many conventions as you can in your area, and at least one per year that requires traveling. Buy the other authors and editors drinks, put a QR code on your shirt with your author logo or slogan/brand, buy books, sell books, and hand out bookmarks with a QR code or even chapbooks. Where does the QR code go? Hopefully to something free where you can also capture emails. Remember, you're a unique individual with a unique voice/brand, so put your own flavor into your marketing.

Interactive Launch Events

Consider hosting live virtual events, Q&A sessions, or interactive webinars where readers can engage with you directly. Invite a few author friends along and do an online panel. These events can create a sense of involvement and personal connection with your audience and fellow authors. For your online launch party, host smaller events leading up to it, or weekly live chats on Facebook, etc. Offer up prizes. Perhaps even a few signed books from other authors, if you're willing to do the same for them. Make your book launches fun for you and your fans. You've successfully written a book instead of just saying you want to. It's something to celebrate.

Reader Involvement

Encourage reader participation by incorporating their input into your work, such as naming characters in upcoming books or choosing cover designs through polls. This not only increases engagement but also makes your readers feel like a part of the creative process. Remember those mailing lists we talked about in *Shadows & Ink Vol. 1*? Stay in touch with them and use that list more and more as the launch approaches. Then again on launch day and less and less after that, asking for reviews and feedback, asking if they'd be interested in a sequel, and sending updates on what you're writing now. After that, email your mailing list at least once a month until you've got another launch coming up. Don't underestimate launch teams (also known as street teams), where readers become part of your launch and share reviews on Amazon, Goodreads, and active Facebook groups. They can even go to local bookstores and start asking that they order your book. Launch teams have never been as influential as they are now, especially with TikTok and Instagram.

Leveraging Analytics and Data

In the digital age, understanding and utilizing data can provide valuable insights into your audience and the effectiveness of your marketing strategies.

- Analytics Tools: Use analytics tools available on social media platforms, your website, and your email marketing service to track engagement, reach, and conversion rates. Do A/B testing with your ads and even email campaigns, testing different calls to action, email subject line, etc.) This data can help you refine your marketing strategies and better target your audience.

- Market Research: Stay informed about trends in the horror genre and publishing industry. Understanding market dynamics can help you position your book effectively and identify new opportunities for growth.

Long-Term Brand Building

A successful writing career is built on a strong, recognizable brand that resonates with your target audience.

- Consistent Branding: Ensure that your branding is consistent across all platforms, from your social media profiles to your book covers.

A cohesive brand image helps readers easily recognize your work and fosters a sense of familiarity and loyalty.

- Personal Storytelling: Share your journey, challenges, and successes with your readers. Authentic storytelling can humanize your brand and build a deeper connection with your audience. Allow yourself to be open, vulnerable, and honest. Control how much you let them in, though. Always be in control.

Innovative Marketing Techniques

Stay ahead of the curve by adopting innovative marketing techniques and exploring new platforms and technologies.

- Augmented Reality (AR) and Virtual Reality (VR): Explore the potential of AR and VR for immersive book experiences, such as virtual book readings or interactive story elements that readers can explore.

- Partnerships and Collaborations: Collaborate with authors, influencers, and brands that align with your genre and brand. Partnerships can open up new channels for exposure and introduce your work to new audiences.

Continuous Learning and Adaptation:

- The publishing industry is ever-evolving, and staying informed about new trends, technologies, and marketing strategies is crucial for sustained success.

- Professional Development: Invest in your professional development by attending workshops, webinars, and conferences focused on writing, marketing, and publishing. Continuous learning will keep your skills sharp and your strategies fresh.

- Adaptability: Be willing to adapt your strategies based on feedback, performance data, and industry trends. Flexibility and a willingness to experiment can lead to innovative approaches that set you apart in a crowded market.

Cross-Promotion with Other Works

Use your book launch as an opportunity to cross-promote your other works. Bundling books, offering discounts on previous titles, or creating box sets can introduce new readers to your broader catalog.

What to Try Right Now:

Use BookFunnel to offer a lead magnet to capture emails, and run a Facebook ad at the bare minimum amount allowed. Let it run for at least three months. Better yet, create five ads for the same lead magnet. Let them run for a week and then choose the one that converts the best, or the one that costs the least per click. Every book should have a budget, but your mailing list should have a permanent monthly budget. Send info via the newsletter at least once per month, with updates, excerpts, behind-the-scenes content, artwork, personal messages, contests, giveaways, etc. Ads that focus directly on books don't normally make a profit, unless you have an upsell, like book 2 in the series. Definitely include an upsell in a non-fiction book to ensure profit for your ads. Don't expect to make a profit from ads for a one-off novel. The upsell for you will be Amazon rankings/visibility, bragging rights if you reach a number 1 spot, reviews, and if you're doing it right, capturing those emails for your next book. Now is also the time to run AMS and BookBub ads.

The journey from a book launch to establishing a long-term writing career is filled with opportunities for growth, engagement, and creative exploration. By building a strong community, strategically planning your content releases, leveraging data, and continuously adapting to the changing landscape, you can create a lasting impact in the horror genre and beyond. Remember, each book launch is not just an end but a stepping stone to greater achievements in your writing career.

> *"Because writing is a solitary craft and we're often off building fantastical worlds in our offices or trapped somewhere in our heads, I've found that it's incredibly important to make sure I get out in the real world (and often, when I can). Try to meet a friend for coffee, or maybe go browse a bookstore and see what some of the new trends are. I'm not always up for socializing, per se, but I do know that barricading myself in my office for weeks on end isn't a good look for me. And while social media is great, especially for connecting with long-distance friends and colleagues--it's also important to breathe some fresh air and be present in what's happening outside your front door.*
> **—Stephanie M. Wytovich**

Chapter 4

Health

In the pursuit of writing excellence, the integration of advanced mind-body techniques is an invaluable aspect of a writer's toolkit. Crafting compelling prose demands not just mental acuity but also a harmonious synchrony between mind and body. Engaging in mindfulness meditation, adopting deep-breathing exercises, and practicing yoga can significantly bolster a writer's focus and creativity. The following guide presents strategies for writers to implement these techniques into their daily routines and to track their effectiveness over time.

Mindfulness Meditation for Writers

Mindfulness meditation is a practice that writers can use to center their thoughts and clear their minds, creating a prime state for writing. To begin, dedicate a quiet space for meditation, free from interruptions and ambient noise. Select a comfortable cushion or chair that supports an upright posture, allowing for unhindered breathing.

Start with a short 5 to 10-minute session, gradually increasing the duration as you become more accustomed to the practice. The key is consistency; thus, integrate this into your daily routine, perhaps at the start of your day or as a break between writing sessions. As you meditate, focus on the present moment, observing your thoughts and emotions without judgment. When your attention drifts, gently guide it back to your breath or a chosen focal point. This practice helps in cultivating mental clarity and patience, which are essential for the sometimes arduous task of writing.

Deep-Breathing Exercises to Enhance Focus

Deep-breathing exercises are a quick and efficient way to reduce stress and improve concentration. Intersperse these exercises throughout your writing day, especially during moments of frustration or mental fatigue. A simple technique is the 4-7-8 method, which involves inhaling for four seconds, holding the breath for seven seconds, and exhaling for eight seconds. This rhythmic breathing induces a sense of calm and can be repeated several times to help refocus your mind.

Incorporate these breathing exercises before tackling a challenging piece of writing or when transitioning between tasks. Over time, you will notice a decrease in stress levels and an increase in your ability to concentrate on the task at hand.

Yoga for Focus and Creativity

Yoga offers physical and mental benefits that are particularly conducive to writing. Its emphasis on flexibility, strength, and balance has parallels in the cognitive flexibility, emotional strength, and balance between work and rest that writers require. Establish a short, daily yoga routine that targets areas of the body commonly affected by prolonged writing, such as the back, neck, and shoulders.

There are specific yoga poses that are beneficial for writers, like the 'Cat-Cow' for spinal flexibility or 'Child's Pose' for relaxation. 'Eagle Arms' is excellent for releasing tension in the shoulder blades, while 'Forward Fold' alleviates lower back stress. Incorporating such poses for even 15 minutes a day can make a significant difference in your writing posture and mental state.

Documenting Your Progress

To truly appreciate the impact of these mind-body techniques, it's vital to maintain a journal documenting your progress. Note the date, time, and details of your meditation, breathing exercises, and yoga practice. Additionally, record your emotional state and any notable effects on your writing performance. Perhaps you'll find that your meditation sessions lead to clearer thought patterns, or that yoga stimulates a burst of creativity.

Observe the direct correlation between your mind-body practices and the quality of your writing. Over weeks and months, look for patterns and adjust your routines accordingly. Maybe longer meditation sessions improve your focus, or perhaps morning yoga invigorates your writing.

By engaging diligently in mindfulness meditation, deep-breathing exercises, and yoga, you, as a writer, can elevate your craft to new heights. Through conscious effort and reflection, you'll discover the unique rhythm that harmonizes your mind and body, paving the way for a more focused, creative writing experience.

In the pursuit of writing excellence, the integration of advanced mind-body techniques is an invaluable aspect of a writer's toolkit. Crafting compelling prose demands not just mental acuity but also a harmonious synchrony between mind and body. Engaging in mindfulness meditation, adopting deep-breathing exercises, and practicing yoga can significantly bolster a writer's focus and creativity. The following guide presents strategies for writers to implement these techniques into their daily routines and to track their effectiveness over time.

Mindfulness Meditation for Writers

Mindfulness meditation is a practice that writers can use to center their thoughts and clear their minds, creating a prime state for writing. To begin, dedicate a quiet space for meditation, free from interruptions and ambient noise. Select a comfortable cushion or chair that supports an upright posture, allowing for unhindered breathing.

Start with a short 5 to 10-minute session, gradually increasing the duration as you become more accustomed to the practice. The key is consistency; thus, integrate this into your daily routine, perhaps at the start of your day or as a break between writing sessions. As you meditate, focus on the present moment, observing your thoughts and emotions without judgment. When your attention drifts, gently guide it back to your breath or a chosen focal point. This practice helps in cultivating mental clarity and patience, which are essential for the sometimes arduous task of writing.

Deep-Breathing Exercises to Enhance Focus

Deep-breathing exercises are a quick and efficient way to reduce stress and improve concentration. Intersperse these exercises throughout your writing day, especially during moments of frustration or mental fatigue. A simple technique is the 4-7-8 method, which involves inhaling for four seconds, holding the breath for seven seconds, and exhaling for eight seconds. This rhythmic breathing induces a sense of calm and can be repeated several times to help refocus your mind.

Incorporate these breathing exercises before tackling a challenging piece of writing or when transitioning between tasks. Over time, you will notice a decrease in stress levels and an increase in your ability to concentrate on the task at hand.

Yoga offers physical and mental benefits that are particularly conducive to writing. Its emphasis on flexibility, strength, and balance has parallels in the cognitive flexibility, emotional strength, and balance between work and rest that writers require. Establish a short, daily yoga routine that targets areas of the body commonly affected by prolonged writing, such as the back, neck, and shoulders.

There are specific yoga poses that are beneficial for writers, like the 'Cat-Cow' for spinal flexibility or 'Child's Pose' for relaxation. 'Eagle Arms' is excellent for releasing tension in the shoulder blades, while 'Forward Fold' alleviates lower back stress. Incorporating such poses for even 15 minutes a day can make a significant difference in your writing posture and mental state.

Documenting Your Progress

To truly appreciate the impact of these mind-body techniques, it's vital to maintain a journal documenting your progress. Note the date, time, and details of your meditation, breathing exercises, and yoga practice. Additionally, record your emotional state and any notable effects on your writing performance. Perhaps you'll find that your meditation sessions lead to clearer thought patterns, or that yoga stimulates a burst of creativity.

Observe the direct correlation between your mind-body practices and the quality of your writing. Over weeks and months, look for patterns and adjust your routines accordingly. Maybe longer meditation sessions improve your focus, or perhaps morning yoga invigorates your writing.

By engaging diligently in mindfulness meditation, deep-breathing exercises, and yoga, you, as a writer, can elevate your craft to new heights. Through conscious effort and reflection, you'll discover the unique rhythm that harmonizes your mind and body, paving the way for a more focused, creative writing experience.

A comprehensive evaluation of a writer's workspace is imperative to achieving an ergonomic setup that can elevate productivity while also safeguarding health. With the growing recognition of the importance of ergonomics for individuals who spend significant time at their desks, such as writers, there has been an influx of advanced ergonomic products designed to optimize the writing environment.

Understanding Ergonomic Efficiency

Ergonomic efficiency is rooted in the science of designing a workspace to fit the user's needs, thereby enhancing comfort and reducing the risk of strain or injury. For writers, this includes the proper arrangement of desks, chairs, keyboards, and monitors to maintain a posture that's as natural as possible.

Desk Ergonomics: The desk is the centerpiece of a writer's workspace. An ergonomic desk should allow for a comfortable reach to all necessary equipment without necessitating excessive stretching or twisting of the body. A height-adjustable desk is a significant investment, allowing writers to alternate between sitting and standing. Standing intermittently throughout the day alleviates the stress on the spine that comes from prolonged sitting and can help maintain energy levels.

When exploring options, one should consider a desk with programmable height settings for ease of transition and memory presets for quick adjustments. Desks with ample space can help maintain an uncluttered work area, which contributes to both physical and mental well-being. Some advanced models even come equipped with built-in health management systems that remind users to stand or sit after a certain period of time.

Chair Ergonomics: An ergonomic chair is perhaps the most critical component of a writer's workspace. A poorly designed chair can lead to a multitude of discomforts and long-term health issues, including lower back pain, neck strain, and impaired circulation. It's vital to select a chair that offers adjustable lumbar support, armrests, seat depth, and height to suit individual body dimensions.

Several high-quality ergonomic chairs on the market go beyond basic adjustability. Some offer dynamic mechanisms that respond to the user's movements, ensuring constant support regardless of the sitting position. Others come with specialized materials that adapt to the body's contours or have designs that encourage micro-movements, promoting blood flow during extensive writing sessions.

Keyboard and Mouse Considerations: The keyboard and mouse are the writer's primary tools of trade and, as such, should be ergonomically designed to prevent repetitive strain injuries like carpal tunnel syndrome. A split or tented keyboard can help maintain wrists in a neutral position, which is the most natural and least stressful posture.

Similarly, an ergonomic mouse designed to fit the natural curve of the hand can significantly reduce muscle strain in the fingers, hands, and wrists. Look for devices that minimize the need for gripping or extensive movement and consider options like trackballs or vertical mice that offer alternative means of interaction.

Monitor Placement: The position of the computer monitor can profoundly affect a writer's neck and eye strain. The top of the monitor should be at or slightly below eye level to prevent tilting the head up or down. Moreover, the monitor should be about an arm's length away to reduce eye fatigue. For those working with dual monitors, they should be positioned in a way that the screens are contiguous, and the user does not need to repeatedly turn the head.

Lighting and Visual Ergonomics: Lighting plays a significant role in maintaining an ergonomic workspace. Poor lighting can cause eye strain and headaches. Natural lighting is ideal, but when it's not available, invest in lamps that offer adjustable intensity and color temperature. These can mimic natural light and be tailored to different times of the day or specific tasks.

Blue light filters and anti-glare screens are also worth considering, especially for writers who work late into the night. These filters can help reduce eye strain and prevent the disruption of sleep patterns associated with excessive exposure to blue light.

Workspace Accessories: In addition to the primary pieces of furniture and equipment, several accessories can further optimize an ergonomic writing environment. A footrest can support the legs and lower back, especially if the feet do not rest comfortably on the ground. A document holder positioned at the same height as the monitor can reduce neck movement and strain when referencing printed material.

Professional Assessment and Personal Adjustments: While there are general guidelines for creating an ergonomic workspace, individual needs may vary. It is wise to consult with an ergonomics professional who can provide a tailored assessment and recommendations. However, small personal adjustments can also make a significant difference. The angle of your chair, the height of your monitor, or the placement of your keyboard should be fine-tuned until you feel comfortable and supported throughout your writing endeavors.

Ergonomics is an ongoing investment in your health and writing career. Evaluate your current setup, research the latest ergonomic advancements, and make informed decisions on which products and practices can best serve your needs. Remember that even the most advanced ergonomic equipment can only be effective if used correctly; therefore, education on optimal ergonomic practices is equally important as the physical tools themselves. With an ergonomic-friendly workspace, a writer can look forward to improved well-being and enhanced productivity, providing a sound foundation for a successful creative process.

Diet

To ensure cognitive function is operating at its peak, writers should be mindful of their diet's impact on their mental clarity, focus, and output. Nutrition plays a pivotal role in brain health, with certain nutrients having a direct influence on cognitive processes such as memory, concentration, and the ability to think clearly. Here are key dietary components that writers should consider integrating into their meal plans for optimal cognitive enhancement.

1. Omega-3 Fatty Acids: Omega-3s, particularly EPA and DHA, are essential for maintaining the structure and function of the brain. These fatty acids are components of neuronal cell membranes and are instrumental in facilitating communication between brain cells. Research has shown that omega-3s can help protect against cognitive decline and may enhance memory and learning. Fatty fish such as salmon, mackerel, and sardines are excellent sources of omega-3s. For vegetarians or individuals who do not consume fish, flaxseeds, chia seeds, walnuts, and algae-based supplements can be valuable alternatives.

2. Antioxidants: Antioxidants help fight oxidative stress, which is linked to age-related cognitive decline. Foods rich in antioxidants such as blueberries, strawberries, dark chocolate, and leafy greens like kale and spinach, can be beneficial. Blueberries, in particular, have been associated with improvements in memory and cognitive function, and they are easy to incorporate into meals, such as in smoothies or as a snack.

3. Complex Carbohydrates: Glucose is the primary source of energy for the brain, and complex carbohydrates provide a steady release of glucose into the bloodstream. This ensures a consistent energy supply to the brain, preventing the spikes and crashes associated with simple sugars. Whole grains, oats, quinoa,

and starchy vegetables are excellent sources of complex carbohydrates. Including a serving of these in each meal can support sustained mental energy throughout the day.

4. B Vitamins: Several B vitamins, including B6, B12, and folic acid, have roles in brain health. They are involved in the production of neurotransmitters, such as serotonin and dopamine, which influence mood and cognitive function. Deficiencies in these vitamins have been linked to depression and cognitive impairment. Foods like lean meats, eggs, dairy products, and leafy greens are high in B vitamins. For those on plant-based diets, fortified cereals and nutritional yeast can provide these essential nutrients.

5. Amino Acids: Amino acids from protein are the building blocks of neurotransmitters. Tryptophan, for example, is a precursor to serotonin, a neurotransmitter that affects mood, sleep, and cognition. Foods rich in tryptophan include turkey, eggs, cheese, and seeds such as pumpkin and chia. Ensuring a balanced intake of amino acids through diverse protein sources can support neurotransmitter synthesis for optimal brain function.

6. Choline: Choline is a critical component of acetylcholine, a neurotransmitter important for memory and learning. Egg yolks are a rich source of choline, and other sources include meat, fish, and dairy products. For those who are vegan or have dietary restrictions, soy products and cruciferous vegetables like broccoli can help meet choline requirements.

7. Polyphenols: Polyphenols have been shown to cross the blood-brain barrier, potentially protecting brain cells from damage and promoting brain health. Foods such as green tea, olive oil, and turmeric contain polyphenols. Turmeric, which contains the active compound curcumin, has received attention for its anti-inflammatory properties and potential to improve cognitive function.

8. Water: Hydration is often overlooked when considering cognitive function. Dehydration can lead to brain fog and difficulty concentrating. It is essential to drink enough water throughout the day, as even mild dehydration can impact cognitive performance.

9. Probiotics and Prebiotics: The gut-brain axis is a communication network between the gut and the brain, which is influenced by the gut microbiota. Probiotics (beneficial bacteria) and prebiotics (food for these bacteria) can positively affect this communication, potentially improving mental clarity and mood. Fermented foods like yogurt, kefir, and kombucha provide probiotics, while fibers found in fruits, vegetables, and whole grains serve as prebiotics.

Writers can consult with a nutritionist to help tailor a meal plan that incorporates these nutrients effectively. This personalized approach can address individual dietary preferences and needs, ensuring a balanced and sustainable diet. Monitoring the effects of dietary changes can be as simple as keeping a food journal alongside a record of mental performance metrics such as focus duration, idea generation, and perceived mental clarity. Over time, this empirical approach can reveal patterns and highlight the specific dietary changes that contribute most significantly to enhancing the writing process.

Mental Health

Writers focus on improving their cognitive abilities through diet, it's equally important to recognize the connection between mental health and the creative process. Writing is often a solitary activity, which can impact a writer's mental health and emotional well-being. Strategies for managing stress, anxiety, and depression are critical for a sustainable writing career. Techniques such as cognitive-behavioral therapy (CBT), counseling, and peer support groups can provide writers with the emotional tools they need to navigate the highs and lows of their creative journey.

When it comes to mental health and emotional well-being, identifying personal stressors is a pivotal step for writers who wish to maintain a healthy balance between their work and personal lives. Writing is an introspective process that often requires deep thought and prolonged periods of solitude. While this can be a rewarding endeavor, it can also give rise to unique mental health challenges such as stress, anxiety, and periods of depression. These emotional states can hinder the creative process, making it imperative for writers to recognize and address their stressors.

Identification of Personal Stressors

The process begins with introspection, as writers must identify what specifically about their writing or personal life is causing tension. Stressors can come from a variety of sources including, but not limited to, tight deadlines, financial pressures, fear of rejection or criticism, or even the content of the writing itself, which may be emotionally taxing. There could also be external stressors such as caregiving responsibilities, relationship issues, or other career obligations. It's important for writers to take stock of these stressors and acknowledge their impact. Keeping a journal can be a helpful way to track mood changes and stress levels in relation to writing and daily activities.

Seeking Mental Health Resources

Once stressors have been identified, the next step is to actively seek out mental health resources. Mental health professionals, such as psychologists and counselors, are trained to help individuals develop coping strategies for dealing with stress and emotional turmoil. Therapy can provide a safe space for writers to explore their feelings, receive guidance, and work through any mental health challenges they are facing.

In addition to one-on-one therapy, there are various types of group therapy and support groups specifically for writers. Organizations such as the Insecure Writers' Support Group and Writers Helping Writers offer communal spaces where writers can share experiences and support each other. These groups understand the unique pressures faced by writers and can offer solidarity and understanding, reducing feelings of isolation.

Online platforms like BetterHelp and Talkspace offer virtual therapy services, making it easier for writers who may have irregular schedules or prefer the privacy of their own space to access professional help. National organizations, such as Mental Health America, provide extensive resources for anyone looking for mental health information and support.

Engaging in Regular Emotional Wellness Practices

Engagement in regular emotional wellness practices is key to maintaining mental health. Mindfulness and meditation are effective methods for writers to manage stress and anxiety. By practicing mindfulness, writers can learn to stay present and grounded, reducing worry about past events or future uncertainties that can distract from the creative process.

Exercise is another crucial wellness practice, as physical activity releases endorphins, which have mood-boosting properties. Even a brief walk can invigorate the mind and provide a much-needed break from the writing desk. Yoga combines physical exercise with meditation and can be particularly beneficial for writers by enhancing flexibility, improving concentration, and promoting relaxation.

Creative expression in other forms, such as painting, cooking, or playing an instrument, can also serve as an outlet for emotional wellness. These activities can provide a reprieve from writing, allowing writers to return to their work refreshed and with a new perspective.

Lastly, establishing a routine that includes time for work as well as relaxation and social interaction can help writers maintain a sense of balance. Scheduling specific times for writing, exercise, leisure, and social activities can provide structure and prevent overwork, which is often a major stressor for writers.

For writers dealing with more serious mental health conditions like depression or anxiety disorders, it's crucial to consult with a healthcare provider to explore treatment options which may include medication, cognitive-behavioral therapy, or other specialized interventions. Remember that mental health is just as important as physical health, and seeking assistance is a sign of strength, not weakness.

Engaging with Nature and Environment

In addition to the aforementioned strategies, the role of nature and environment in supporting mental health cannot be understated. Spending time outdoors, surrounded by natural beauty, can have a calming effect and inspire creative thought. The sounds, sights, and smells of nature can refresh the mind and improve mood. Writers should consider incorporating outdoor time into their daily routine, whether it's taking a short walk in a local park or finding a quiet place to write outside. Studies have shown that even viewing scenes of nature can reduce stress and anxiety, making it worthwhile to create a workspace with views of the outdoors or images of natural landscapes.

Moreover, biophilic design, which incorporates natural elements into indoor spaces, can be integrated into a writer's workspace. Indoor plants, natural light, and materials that mimic nature can help create a serene and inspiring writing environment. These elements not only improve mental well-being but can also enhance creativity and productivity.

Writers often overlook the impact of their physical environment on their mental health. Yet, creating a space that is conducive to writing and emotionally supportive can make a significant difference. This could mean setting up a dedicated writing area that is clutter-free, comfortable, and personalized with inspirational quotes or artwork. It's also important to ensure that the space is free from distractions that can cause stress or interrupt the flow of writing.

Social Wellness and Community Engagement

Finally, social wellness and community engagement are essential for writers' emotional health. Engaging with fellow writers and participating in the larger writing community can provide a sense of belonging and decrease feelings of loneliness or isolation. Whether it's through online forums, local writing groups, or attending writing conferences and retreats, connecting with others who share similar interests and challenges can be incredibly affirming.

It's important for writers to foster relationships not just within the writing community but also in their personal lives. Maintaining friendships and family connections can provide emotional support and a different perspective on life, enriching the writer's own experiences and thus their writing. Volunteering and participating in community activities can also contribute to a writer's social wellness by providing a sense of purpose and connection to others.

By identifying personal stressors, utilizing mental health resources, and engaging in regular emotional wellness practices, writers can manage their mental health effectively. This holistic approach to well-being supports not just their craft but their overall quality of life, ensuring that they can continue to produce their best work without sacrificing their mental health.

Optimizing Sleep Science for Writers

Sleep is a crucial component of a writer's life, influencing cognitive abilities, mood, and overall health. The process of writing demands high levels of mental energy and clarity, and without adequate rest, writers can find themselves struggling with concentration, creativity, and productivity. This is where the science of sleep can greatly impact a writer's routine and output.

Examination of Current Sleep Habits

To harness the benefits of sleep, writers must first evaluate their existing sleep habits. Monitoring sleep involves assessing not just the duration but also the quality of sleep. Keeping a sleep diary can be an enlightening exercise, where writers record the time they go to bed, the estimated time it takes to fall asleep, the number of awakenings during the night, wake-up time, and the overall quality of sleep. This log should be kept consistently for at least a week to identify patterns and issues, such as irregular sleep schedules or frequent disturbances.

Best Practices from Sleep Science:
- The field of sleep science provides an array of best practices to establish an optimal sleep routine. Here are several key recommendations that writers can integrate into their lives:

- Consistent Sleep Schedule: A regular sleep-wake cycle aligns with the body's internal clock, known as the circadian rhythm. Going to bed and waking up at the same time every day, even on weekends, can improve sleep quality and help avoid the grogginess of sleep inertia.

- Pre-Sleep Routine: Establishing a pre-sleep routine signals the body that it's time to wind down. This may include activities such as reading (preferably not on a screen), meditating, or practicing relaxation exercises. Such activities can facilitate the transition into sleep.

- Optimize Sleep Environment: The bedroom should be conducive to rest. This means maintaining a cool, quiet, and dark environment.

Using blackout curtains, earplugs, or a white noise machine can help create the ideal conditions for uninterrupted sleep.

- Limit Exposure to Blue Light: Screens emit blue light, which can interfere with the production of the sleep hormone melatonin. Writers should limit the use of electronic devices before bedtime or use blue light filters to mitigate the impact.

- Moderate Afternoon Naps: While napping can be beneficial, particularly for those who are sleep-deprived, long naps or napping late in the day can disrupt night-time sleep. A short, 20-minute power nap can be refreshing without affecting the night's sleep cycle.

- Monitor Caffeine and Alcohol Intake: Both substances can adversely affect sleep. Caffeine, a stimulant, can keep writers awake if consumed too late in the day, while alcohol, although initially sedating, can lead to fragmented sleep.

- Physical Activity: Regular exercise can contribute to better sleep. However, intense workouts close to bedtime may lead to increased alertness, so it's best to schedule exercise sessions earlier in the day.

- Diet and Sleep: Eating large meals or spicy foods shortly before bedtime can cause discomfort and indigestion, affecting sleep quality. Light snacks are preferable if hunger strikes close to bedtime.

Monitoring Sleep Quality and Impact on Writing:

After implementing these practices, writers should continue to monitor their sleep and reflect on any changes in their writing performance. Tracking cognitive functions like memory, attention span, and problem-solving abilities can provide insights into the benefits of optimized sleep. For instance, on days following good sleep, writers may notice enhanced vocabulary recall and fluidity in their prose, while poor sleep may correlate with sluggish thinking and a lack of motivation.

Sophisticated devices like sleep trackers or smartwatches can provide detailed analyses such as sleep duration, sleep stages (REM, light, and deep sleep), and sleep disruptions. However, these should be used as tools for general guidance rather than precise medical assessments.

In practice, writers may find that sleep optimization is a dynamic process. It may take several weeks of trial and adjustment to establish the best sleep routine. Being attuned to one's body and its responses to different sleep strategies is key to determining what works best on an individual basis.

It's important to note that persistent sleep issues or disturbances may signify underlying health conditions, such as insomnia or sleep apnea. In such cases, it is essential to consult with a healthcare professional.

Optimizing sleep is a fundamental aspect of supporting the creative process. A well-rested writer is better positioned to harness their full potential, turning the dream of eloquent prose into reality. By incorporating the science of sleep into their routine, writers not only improve their work but also contribute to their overall well-being.

The nexus between the natural world and the creative faculties of a writer is one that has long been celebrated and romanticized in literature and beyond. For writers, nature offers not just a scenic backdrop but a source of profound stimulation for the mind and spirit, influencing their creative process in myriad ways. As a writer, by bringing elements of the natural environment into your daily routine or workspace, you can tap into this wellspring of inspiration and rejuvenation to enhance your creative output.

Incorporating Nature into Your Writing Routine

Integrating nature into your writing routine can be as simple or as elaborate as you prefer. One of the easiest ways to start is by planning outdoor writing sessions. Whether it's sitting in a serene park, beside a gently flowing stream, or under the shade of a towering tree, the sensory experience of nature—the sounds, sights, and scents—can act as a catalyst for imagination. The tranquility of these settings provides a respite from the noise of urban life, allowing for clearer thought and a calmer state of mind. Moreover, the change of environment can help dissolve writer's block and generate fresh ideas.

When the weather or circumstances don't permit outdoor excursions, you can still incorporate the essence of nature into your indoor writing space. Positioning your desk near a window with a view of the outdoors creates a visual connection with nature, offering moments of distraction that can be mentally refreshing. Indoor plants, too, can be particularly effective, not just for their aesthetic value but also for their ability to improve air quality and evoke a sense of calm. Consider adding a small fountain or a sound machine that mimics natural sounds like rainfall or ocean waves to enrich the sensory experience even further.

Biophilic Design Principles in the Workspace

To deepen the integration of nature in your workspace, you can employ principles of biophilic design—a concept used in architecture and interior design that seeks to connect building occupants more closely to nature. This involves more than just adding plants; it encompasses a variety of strategies, such as maximizing natural light, using natural materials and colors, and incorporating nature-inspired forms and patterns into your surroundings. For example, using wood for furniture or decor can evoke the essence of a forest, while images or paintings of landscapes can serve as a visual escape to the outdoors. These elements not only add a touch of nature to your workspace but also serve to create a sense of well-being and creativity.

Physical and Psychological Benefits

The benefits of surrounding oneself with nature go beyond mere aesthetics. Research has shown that exposure to natural environments can have a range of positive impacts on physical and mental health. For instance, natural light has been found to elevate mood and improve sleep quality by regulating circadian rhythms. The presence of plants can reduce stress levels, enhance concentration, and increase productivity—all crucial advantages for the demanding work of writing.

In addition to health benefits, nature can fuel creativity by providing a rich tapestry of stimuli that can be woven into the fabric of one's writing. Nature is replete with metaphorical possibilities and can serve as an inexhaustible source of sensory detail, deepening the descriptiveness and emotional resonance of prose. Furthermore, the contemplative aspect of nature can facilitate profound reflection, often leading to breakthroughs in narrative structure and character development.

Cultivating a Mindful Relationship with Nature

As important as it is to physically surround oneself with nature, cultivating a mindful relationship with the environment is equally beneficial. Mindfulness practices, such as walking meditations in a natural setting, can deepen your connection to the present moment and to the intricate details of the environment. These practices not only foster a greater appreciation of the natural world but can also become a fertile ground for germinating ideas and themes that can be explored in your writing.

Documenting the Influence of Nature

To truly appreciate the impact of nature on your writing, consider keeping a nature journal. Document not just your observations of the natural world but also how these observations influence your thoughts, emotions, and writing. Over time, you might find recurring themes or insights that can be developed into larger works. Furthermore, regularly reviewing your nature journal entries can provide a wellspring of material to draw from when you find yourself in need of inspiration.

In summary, the deliberate incorporation of nature into your daily routine and workspace is not just a means of seeking inspiration; it's an acknowledgment of the symbiotic relationship between your inner creative landscape and the outer natural world. This connection can act as a powerful conduit, enhancing your writing with the vitality and harmony that nature inherently possesses. Engaging with nature, therefore, becomes an essential aspect of nurturing your creative process, enabling you to produce work that is as rich and dynamic as the environment that inspires it.

In the life of a writer, seeking out and engaging with writing communities holds great value, both for personal development and professional advancement. These communities serve as a conduit through which writers can build connections, gain new perspectives, and find inspiration. Whether it's the warmth of local gatherings or the broad reach of online forums, every interaction has the potential to enrich a writer's craft and creative spirit.

Local writing communities offer a wealth of opportunities for writers looking to engage with peers in a face-to-face setting. Cities and towns often host a variety of writing groups that meet regularly at libraries, bookstores, coffee shops, or other communal spaces. These groups may focus on specific genres such as poetry, fiction, nonfiction, or screenwriting, or they might be more general in their scope, welcoming writers across all genres and levels of experience. Such local groups often create a supportive environment where members can share their work, offer and receive constructive criticism, and discuss the challenges and triumphs of the writing process.

The benefits of participating in these local groups are manifold. The immediacy of face-to-face feedback provides immediate insights into the impact of one's writing. Furthermore, regular meetings help in establishing a routine and accountability that can be difficult to maintain in isolation. Writers often find that being part of a local community gives them a sense of belonging and the motivation to keep honing their craft. Many local groups also host guest speakers, readings, and writing workshops, allowing members to learn from more experienced writers and industry professionals.

Networking events specifically designed for writers should not be overlooked. These events can range from informal mixers to formal conferences and seminars. They are excellent venues for meeting a diverse array of industry professionals including publishers, literary agents, and editors. Making connections at such events can lead to valuable partnerships, mentorship opportunities, and, occasionally, the chance to pitch work to industry gatekeepers. They also serve as a barometer for current market trends and provide insight into the business side of writing, an aspect that is crucial for any writer looking to publish their work.

Engagement with online writing communities presents a different set of advantages. The digital age has allowed writers from all corners of the world to connect and collaborate like never before. There are numerous online forums, social media groups, and writing platforms where individuals can participate in discussions, share their work, and receive feedback from a global audience. The asynchronous nature of these online communities means that writers can engage at times that suit their schedules, a level of flexibility that local groups may not always provide.

Online platforms often host writing challenges, virtual workshops, and webinars that can be accessed from the comfort of one's home. These activities can be especially beneficial for those who live in areas with fewer in-person writing resources or for those who prefer the digital medium for interaction. Additionally, online communities are fertile grounds for diverse perspectives, exposing writers to a wider range of voices and storytelling techniques than they may encounter locally.

To maximize the benefits of participation in both local and online writing communities, writers should approach them with a spirit of openness and a willingness to contribute. Networking is a two-way street; offering support and insight to others can be just as rewarding as receiving it. Writers who actively participate by reading and commenting on others' work, sharing opportunities, and celebrating each other's successes often find that they gain the most from these communities.

Furthermore, attending workshops, whether in person or online, can be a transformative experience for a writer. Workshops often focus on honing specific skills, such as character development, plot structure, or dialogue. They are led by experienced writers or educators who can provide in-depth analysis and guidance that writers can apply to their own work. The workshop setting also encourages the development of critical thinking about one's writing and the craft as a whole.

In conclusion, becoming an active member of writing communities and participating in workshops and networking events is a powerful strategy for personal and professional growth. By building connections with fellow writers and industry professionals, seeking feedback, and continuing to learn, writers enrich their craft and widen their horizons. The support and camaraderie found in these circles can be a source of strength, helping writers to navigate the often solitary path of the writing journey with resilience and confidence.

Holistic Approaches

Holistic health practices offer a comprehensive approach to wellness that considers the entire person—body, mind, and spirit. By integrating these practices into one's routine, writers can experience benefits that enhance their overall well-being and creativity. Let's delve into a range of holistic health modalities that can support a writer's journey to creative longevity.

Acupuncture: Acupuncture is an ancient Chinese healing technique involving the insertion of very thin needles through the skin at strategic points on the body. This practice is based on the concept of balancing the flow of energy, or Qi (pronounced "chee"), through pathways known as meridians. Writers can utilize acupuncture to relieve stress, alleviate pain, improve sleep, and enhance focus—all of which contribute to a more productive writing practice. Regular sessions with a licensed acupuncturist could lead to increased energy levels and improved mood, fostering a conducive environment for creativity.

Aromatherapy: Utilizing essential oils extracted from flowers, herbs, and trees, aromatherapy works through the sense of smell and skin absorption. It is proposed that the scents from essential oils can stimulate the limbic system, the part of the brain responsible for emotions, behavior, and long-term memory. For writers, aromatherapy may be particularly beneficial when combating mental fatigue, stimulating creativity, or setting a mood for specific writing tasks. Diffusing oils such as lavender for relaxation or peppermint for alertness during writing sessions can positively influence mood and creative output.

Herbal Medicine: Herbal medicine employs plant-based remedies for therapeutic purposes. Herbs such as ginkgo biloba for cognitive enhancement or St. John's Wort for mood stabilization have been subjects of study for their potential health benefits. By incorporating certain herbs into one's diet—under the guidance of a qualified herbalist or healthcare provider—writers can support their cognitive functions and emotional health. It is crucial to note that some herbs can interact with prescription medications, so it's important to consult with a professional before beginning any herbal regimen.

Tai Chi and Qigong: These gentle practices combine movement, meditation, and rhythmic breathing to foster a state of relaxation and improved health. Tai Chi and Qigong are often referred to as moving meditations, ideal for writers who spend long hours seated. By participating in Tai Chi or Qigong, writers can improve their flexibility, balance, and overall body awareness. These practices can also enhance mental clarity and emotional tranquility, which are invaluable for a writer's creative process.

Yoga and Meditation: Yoga integrates physical postures, breathing techniques, and meditation to promote physical and mental well-being. Writers can utilize yoga to reduce tension in the body, which is especially beneficial for those experiencing discomfort from prolonged sitting. Meditation, on the other hand, encourages a state of restful awareness and has been shown to reduce stress and anxiety. When used in combination, yoga and meditation can improve a writer's concentration and open the mind to new creative possibilities.

Chiropractic Care: Chiropractic care focuses on disorders of the musculoskeletal system and the nervous system, often through spinal adjustments. Writers experiencing back pain, neck stiffness, or repetitive strain injuries may find relief through chiropractic treatments. Improved spinal alignment can enhance nerve function, potentially leading to heightened mental clarity and reduced physical discomfort, thus enabling longer and more productive writing sessions.

Reiki: Reiki is a form of energy healing originating from Japan. It involves the transfer of universal energy from the practitioner's palms to the patient, promoting healing and balance. For writers, Reiki sessions can be a method to alleviate stress, clear emotional blockages, and attain a state of peace. Some

257

individuals report feeling more energetically aligned and creatively inspired following Reiki treatments.

Integrating Holistic Practices

Choosing one or more holistic health practices to integrate into a routine should be a personalized process, taking into account individual preferences, needs, and health conditions. It may be helpful for writers to begin by selecting a single practice and noting any shifts in energy, mood, or creative output over time. By keeping a journal, writers can document their experiences and evaluate the effectiveness of each practice in enhancing their well-being and writing performance.

Monitoring Changes

After incorporating holistic practices into their routine, writers should pay close attention to changes in their physical sensations, emotional states, and creative processes. It might take several sessions or an extended period of consistent practice to notice significant improvements. Writers could track variables such as the number of words written per day, the ease with which ideas flow, the quality of sleep, and overall satisfaction with their writing to determine the impact of holistic health practices on their craft.

By mindfully engaging with holistic health practices, writers can nurture their physical, mental, and emotional well-being, thereby supporting and sustaining their creative endeavors. As with any new health regimen, it's recommended to consult with healthcare professionals to ensure that chosen practices complement one's personal health goals and circumstances. With a holistic approach, writers can lay the foundation for a vibrant and enduring creative life.

Chapter 5

Legal and Ethical Considerations

Horror fiction, a genre that holds a longstanding tradition of chilling the spine and quickening the pulse, has been a staple of cultural expression with roots stretching deep into the history of storytelling. Horror narratives, irrespective of medium—whether oral folklore, literary works, or cinematic productions—have consistently served as a mirror reflecting humanity's darkest fears, moral anxieties, and societal taboos. The genre's predilection for addressing the unspeakable, for confronting the macabre, and for jolting the very nerves of its audience has set it apart from other forms of fiction. Consequently, these attributes have forged a path fraught with complex legal and ethical considerations that are as intricate as the narratives themselves.

Historically, horror has perennially evolved, mirroring the evolving fears and anxieties of society. In ancient folklore and myth, tales of demons, ghouls, and monsters such as the Greek tales of the Minotaur and Medusa served as allegories for universal human fears. In the 18th and 19th centuries, Gothic literature began to emerge with Horace Walpole's *The Castle of Otranto* and Mary Shelley's *Frankenstein*, blending romance and terror to examine the darker aspects of human nature and society. This era paved the way for horror as a recognized genre in literature, intertwining themes of the supernatural with psychological depth.

The 20th century witnessed horror fiction rise in popularity with authors like H.P. Lovecraft and Stephen King, who not only captivated readers with tales of cosmic terror and the macabre but also mastered the art of embodying societal fears in their works. Lovecraft's stories of ancient, indifferent cosmic beings reflected a post-World War I society grappling with its own insignificance, while King's novels often highlight the horrors lurking within everyday life and the human psyche, resonating with various societal fears throughout the decades.

It is horror's inherent ability to invoke intense feelings—from terror to disgust—that situates it within a unique realm of scrutiny. The genre delves into the complexities of human emotion, seeking not only to entertain but also to invoke a cathartic response by engaging with innate fears. This interaction with the reader or viewer's most primal instincts is what sets horror apart and what also calls for a careful navigation of legal and ethical lines. The depiction of the macabre, violence, and taboo subjects in horror has a potent effect that other genres might not achieve with the same intensity. Consequently, these depictions can teeter on the brink of what is considered acceptable by societal standards and legal systems.

The ethical dimension of horror fiction cannot be overstated. Its content often involves scenarios of extreme violence, psychological terror, and at times, real-life horrors that can be deeply affecting. This immersive quality of horror raises questions about the nature of entertainment and its boundaries. When does the depiction of violence serve the story, and when does it cross into gratuitousness? How does a horror narrative balance between providing a safe space to explore fear and contributing to a desensitization to violence or perpetuating harmful stereotypes?

Moreover, horror fiction's enduring popularity and influence necessitates a rigorous analysis of its responsibilities to both readers and society. The genre's exploration of taboo subjects, from sexual deviance to graphic violence, requires authors to tread with caution to avoid gratuitous shocks or the inadvertent glamorization of what should be portrayed with sensitivity. Horror writers, therefore, must often grapple with the moral implications of their work, reflecting on how they engage with the reader's deepest fears while remaining respectful of real-world tragedies and traumas.

These distinctive characteristics of horror fiction set the stage for a complex legal landscape, too. The genre's content, with its frequent nods to prior mythologies and works, calls into question the originality of ideas and the limits of copyright protection. The genre's ability to resonate through shared cultural fears raises concerns about the extent to which horror narratives can draw upon real-life events and figures without infringing upon the rights of individuals or misrepresenting historical truths.

In balancing these various facets—historical context, societal impact, and emotional potency—horror fiction emerges as a genre that must constantly negotiate the fine lines of legality and morality. The next section will explore the specific contours of copyright law as it applies to the artful craft of horror storytelling, probing the safeguards and potential pitfalls that writers and creators must navigate in their work.

Copyright Laws in Horror Fiction

In the chilling corridors of horror fiction, where authors dabble in the dark arts of storytelling, copyright laws play the sentinel role, guarding the precincts of creativity. The meticulous craft of concocting dread and suspense hinges not only on originality but also on the nuanced use of existing myths and motifs. To better understand this intricate interplay, it is essential to examine the role of copyright laws in preserving the integrity of horror authors' original works, the tradition of drawing on communal lore, and the curious case of fair use within this evocative genre.

Copyright laws serve as the bedrock of protection for literary works. Underpinning the rights of authors to exclusively control the use of their original compositions, these laws are designed to incentivize creativity, ensuring that creators can reap the financial benefits and recognition from their intellectual endeavors. In the context of horror fiction, where the imagination unfurls in the form of unique characters, unsettling plots, and haunting settings, copyright serves as a shield against the unauthorized replication of these elements, empowering authors to dictate how their nightmarish creations are disseminated and adapted.

Given that horror, as a genre, is heavily reliant on a shared cultural lexicon of fears and folklore, it stands at a unique crossroads where the protection of individual expression must be balanced with the genre's tradition of communal storytelling. The evocation of vampires, werewolves, and ghosts, for instance, may draw on archetypal figures embedded within the public domain. These entities often lack a single point of origin, having been refined and reinterpreted across generations. As horror fiction weaves new tales from these age-old threads, it demonstrates the delicate dance between original contribution and collective heritage.

This dance raises crucial questions about the boundaries of copyright protection. How does an author establish copyright over a work that interlaces the personal and the impersonal, the freshly conjured and the anciently known? The key lies in the expression of ideas rather than the ideas themselves. Copyright does not guard an idea as ephemeral as 'undead beings with an aversion to sunlight.' Rather, it safeguards the distinctive manner in which a writer articulates this concept, the particular narrative spun around it, and the original characters that populate this vision.

Yet, the path of horror literature is often paved with homage and pastiche, wherein authors pay tribute to or riff on the established works of their predecessors. This is where the doctrine of fair use reveals itself to be of paramount importance to the genre. Fair use is a legal principle that allows limited borrowing from copyrighted materials without the need for permission, under certain conditions. These conditions are typically assessed through factors such as the purpose of the use, the nature of the copyrighted work, the amount and substantiality of the portion taken, and the effect of the use on the potential market for the original work.

In the realm of horror, fair use permits authors to engage in literary commentary, criticism, or parody, drawing from existing works to create something that is transformative and adds new meaning or insights. This transformative nature is crucial—it delineates the distinction between mere replication and innovative reinterpretation. An author of horror fiction, for instance, might use the setting of a known vampire mythos to critically examine contemporary social issues, effectively creating a work that stands apart from the original both in intent and expression.

Nevertheless, the ambiguity inherent in fair use can become a double-edged sword, striking fear into the hearts of horror authors and publishers alike. While fair use intends to balance the rights of original authors with the public interest in fostering artistic dialogue and innovation, its application is often unpredictable, left to the discretion of judicial interpretation. This unpredictability can have a chilling effect on creativity, as authors may shy away from incorporating or referencing existing works out of concern for potential copyright infringement litigation.

The spectral presence of legal battles looms large over horror fiction. Take, for example, the notorious disputes over derivative works and their proximity to the original content that inspired them. The criteria used to determine whether a work is infringing can be as enigmatic as a ghost story. It is not merely the similarity of content that is examined, but also the likelihood of consumer confusion and the possibility that the derivative work could usurp the market of the original. Horror fiction, with its proclivity for reimagining tropes and revitalizing fear in innovative manners, sits at the epicenter of such disputes.

Authors must also navigate the murky waters of what constitutes a substantial part of a work. A single line, a recurring motif, or a complex character might be adjudged as too substantial, tipping the balance away from fair use and toward infringement. For horror authors, who may conjure their terrors from the collective cauldron of cultural myths and literary references, discerning the tipping point can be as fraught as the narratives they craft.

The tension between copyright protection and the genre's tradition of building upon existing stories is not only a legal challenge but also an ethical one. Authors of horror fiction bear the responsibility of honoring the intellectual property of others while fostering the communal storytelling tradition that fuels the genre's continual evolution. As they tread the shadowy line between originality and homage, they engage in an ethical balancing act, ensuring that their works do not unfairly diminish the rights of fellow creators, nor the expectancy of their audiences for fresh, yet familiar, terrains of terror.

The concept of fair use in horror fiction, then, functions as a lantern in the legal labyrinth, providing guidance but no guaranteed safe passage. Authors must wield this light with care, using it to illuminate their paths toward innovation without infringing upon the sacred rights of originality. In doing so, they contribute to the living corpus of horror fiction, a genre that thrives on the delicate interplay of old fears and new frontiers.

As we pull back the shroud on copyright laws in horror fiction, we see a complex, ever-shifting landscape, where authors must be both adept at storytelling and savvy about the legal implications of their craft.

Depiction of Violence and Sensitive Content

The depiction of violence and sensitive content is a prominent feature of horror fiction, serving as a critical element that often defines the genre. This portrayal can be a double-edged sword, capable of eliciting a profound psychological response from the audience while simultaneously risking the venture into realms of gratuitous violence and exploitation. For authors, the challenge is to tread the delicate boundary between invoking terror and inducing revulsion, between creating memorable stories and causing unnecessary distress.

Violence in horror fiction is not merely a conduit for thrill or shock but serves as a narrative tool that can underscore themes such as the vulnerability of the human condition, the existence of evil, and the confrontation with mortality. It often acts as a metaphor for real-world fears and anxieties, providing a cathartic outlet for both the writer and the reader. However, the ethical implications of depicting violence demand careful consideration. Authors need to ask themselves whether the violence is essential to the story and how it contributes to the narrative or the development of characters.

To navigate the fine line between compelling horror and gratuitous violence, writers should aim to ensure that any violent content serves a purpose beyond mere spectacle. This requires a thoughtful approach to storytelling wherein violence is not glorified but presented in a context that adds depth to the story. It may, for instance, highlight the fragility of life, the consequences of immoral actions, or the heroism in the face of danger.

Graphic depictions can have emotional and psychological effects on readers, including triggering past traumas or inciting fear. Writers should, therefore, consider the implementation of trigger warnings as a courtesy to readers. These warnings provide a brief notice about the content that follows, giving readers the chance to decide if they wish to proceed. Although some argue that trigger warnings may dampen the element of surprise inherent to horror, they are a sign of respect for the reader's personal experiences and boundaries.

Another ethical concern is the treatment of sensitive subjects such as sexual assault, torture, and the depiction of harm to vulnerable individuals, including children. These topics must be handled with the utmost sensitivity and should not be included for shock value alone. A good rule of thumb for writers is to consider whether the narrative could be just as impactful without such scenes. If the answer is yes, it may be worth reconsidering their inclusion.

Authors should also be mindful of the potential desensitizing effect that continuous exposure to violence can have on readers. While some readers seek out horror for its ability to explore dark themes in a safe and controlled environment, there is a risk that repeated exposure to graphic content can diminish its impact or, worse, normalize the violence. Therefore, horror writers must carefully balance the frequency and intensity of violent scenes to maintain their effectiveness and avoid desensitizing their audience.

Moreover, responsible storytelling involves reflecting on the consequences of violence within the narrative. It's important for authors to show not just the act of violence but also its repercussions—how it affects the characters, the community, or the story's world. This not only adds a layer of realism to the tale but also emphasizes that actions have consequences, reinforcing the moral complexities of the narrative.

Engaging with ethical considerations also extends to the portrayal of antagonists and victims. Writers should strive to depict their characters as fully realized individuals, rather than mere caricatures or vehicles for violence. This approach encourages a more nuanced understanding of good versus evil and can provoke deeper emotional and intellectual responses from the audience.

Furthermore, horror authors can benefit from ongoing dialogue with their readers and peers about the handling of violence and sensitive content. This interaction can provide valuable feedback on what is considered respectful and what may be crossing the line. It also allows writers to gauge cultural and societal shifts in perceptions of violence and adapt their storytelling accordingly.

Ultimately, writing horror fiction requires a careful balancing act—respecting the genre's conventions of thrill and suspense while handling violent and sensitive content with the ethical consideration it demands. By being mindful of these aspects, writers not only craft more powerful and effective stories but also contribute to the ongoing discourse about the role of violence in media. In doing so, they ensure that their work remains impactful and respected, providing both entertainment and meaningful commentary on the human experience.

Writers' Responsibilities Toward Their Audience

In the labyrinthine world of horror fiction, authors must navigate the murky waters of their responsibilities toward their audience. This duty is multifaceted, encompassing the sensitive deployment of trigger warnings, the ethical imperative to avoid perpetuating harmful stereotypes, and the necessity of honoring audience sensitivities without stifling the creative spirit that gives the genre its lifeblood.

The use of trigger warnings is perhaps one of the more debated topics when it comes to authorial responsibility in horror writing. On one side, critics of trigger warnings argue that they may compromise the suspense and unexpectedness inherent in the horror genre. They claim that warnings could potentially diminish the visceral reactions that are a hallmark of horror's appeal. On the other side are proponents who believe that trigger warnings are a form of empathy, a way for authors to acknowledge that, while they intend to scare, they do not wish to traumatize. This is particularly relevant in a genre that often explores themes of violence, death, and psychological distress, which can resonate differently with each reader based on their personal experiences.

The ethical use of trigger warnings, then, becomes a nuanced exercise in balance. Horror authors must carefully consider the specific content of their work and its potential impact. For instance, explicit scenes of sexual violence, self-harm, or graphic depictions of mental illness might warrant a warning. The objective here is not censorship but to provide readers with the autonomy to engage with the story on their terms, especially if the content might echo personal traumas.

Beyond the consideration of potential triggers, horror authors are tasked with the moral duty of not reinforcing harmful stereotypes or promoting toxic ideologies through their narratives. The genre has historically been criticized for its depiction of characters from marginalized groups in reductive or villainous roles. Female characters, in particular, have often been portrayed as helpless victims or sexualized figures, while characters of color have been relegated to sacrificial roles or portrayed as the exotic 'other'. These depictions can perpetuate stereotypes, entrench biases, and contribute to a culture of misunderstanding and prejudice.

To address this, writers must engage in a critical self-examination of the tropes and narratives they employ. Crafting stories that feature diverse characters with agency and complexity is not only a step toward more ethical storytelling but also enriches the genre. This approach challenges writers to be innovative, to create horror that is as inclusive as it is haunting, and to tell stories that resonate with a broader audience without compromising the integrity of the narrative.

Respecting audience sensitivities, however, does not necessarily equate to pandering or self-censorship. Horror, by its very nature, is meant to probe the boundaries of comfort, to disturb and unsettle. Authors must honor this intention, as it is at the core of what draws many to the genre. The question then becomes how horror writers can present content that is terrifying yet thoughtful, provocative yet considerate of the wider impact such content may have.

One way authors can do this is by ensuring that the representation of violence or other sensitive issues is purposeful and integral to the story. Gratuitous violence or the exploitation of sensitive content for shock value alone can come across as disrespectful and thoughtless. Instead, horror writers can focus on building atmosphere and suspense through subtler means, employing psychological horror and the power of suggestion. The unease that comes from an unexplained noise or the sense of dread that builds from an uncanny situation can be more potent than overt violence. This approach requires a deft hand and a deep understanding of what truly frightens us as humans.

Authors must recognize the power they wield through their words. Just as horror can unsettle, it can also illuminate and elevate. There is a potential for the genre to engage with and explore societal fears, existential questions, and the human condition in meaningful ways. When done with intention and sensitivity, horror fiction can transcend pure entertainment to become a reflective and transformative experience for readers.

In the context of these responsibilities, authors find themselves as custodians of their audience's trust. They are tasked with creating narratives that respect the intelligence and emotional landscape of their readers while also staying true to the essence of horror. It is a juggling act, maintaining the chilling allure that defines horror fiction while also holding fast to ethical storytelling principles.

The interplay of creativity and ethics is, in many ways, the heartbeat of the horror genre. It demands of its authors a constant, mindful calibration of their narratives to ensure they are producing work that is as responsible as it is riveting. This task is as challenging as it is critical. As authors pen their tales of terror, they must remember that the impact of their stories extends beyond the page, shaping not just nightmares but also the very fabric of the reading experience.

Now, as we pivot our examination toward the tension between creative freedom and societal norms, we delve further into the ways horror writers can continue to push the envelope in exploring taboo topics while remaining respectful and socially responsible.

Creative Freedom Versus Societal Norms

The nuanced relationship between creative freedom and adherence to societal norms has long been a contentious issue, particularly in the realm of horror fiction. Authors within this genre wield the unique ability to delve into the darkest recesses of the human psyche, often grappling with themes that challenge the status quo and provoke deep-seated fears. As such, the horror writer becomes a tightrope walker, balancing their imaginative prowess with a conscientious awareness of contemporary societal norms and the potential impact their work might have.

This balance is significant given the nature of horror fiction. It is a genre that inherently explores taboo subjects, subjects that can both fascinate and repulse, such as death, mutilation, the supernatural, and the abject nature of what society deems 'monstrous.' The allure of horror fiction lies in its ability to confront what is normally repressed or left unspoken.

Case Studies: Controversial Horror Works

To explore the balance between freedom of expression and responsible story-telling within the horror genre, we turn to case studies of controversial horror works that have sparked legal battles and ethical debates. These cases illuminate the practical implications of the topics previously discussed and provide salient lessons for authors, publishers, and distributors alike.

One notable case revolves around Clive Barker's Hellraiser franchise, which, while celebrated for its unique vision of horror, has faced its share of legal complications. The character of Pinhead, who has become a cultural icon, was subject to litigation over ownership rights between Barker and the production company. Barker regained rights to the Hellraiser concept in the United States in 2021, emphasizing the importance for creators in understanding copyright agreements and the lasting implications they have on their creations, especially in a medium like horror, where iconic elements can have significant commercial and cultural value.

The ongoing saga of *Friday the 13th* is another case in point, epitomized by the "Horror Inc. v. Miller" case. The lawsuit pertains to the copyright status of the original script and its key elements. Victor Miller, the screenwriter of the first film, claimed authorship and sought to recapture the rights, leading to a complex legal battle with the franchise's producers. The litigation highlights the intricacy of "work for hire" agreements and the delineation of rights when multiple parties contribute to a work over time. The dispute has effectively stalled the creation of new content in the Friday the 13th franchise, demonstrating the extensive impact legal issues can have on the future of horror series and their fans.

In terms of ethical debates, the *Silent Hill 2* video game stands out. Its intense psychological horror and themes of abuse and guilt led to discussions about the portrayal of mental illness and trauma in horror media. The ethical considerations here are manifold: the game challenges the audience to empathize with flawed, even morally compromised characters. While it was lauded for its deep narrative, some criticized it for potentially trivializing serious mental health issues. This case underscores the ethical responsibility creators have in portraying sensitive subjects with due diligence and the nuances involved in eliciting horror through psychological exploration.

The Saw franchise, with its graphic depictions of violence and torture, sparked debate over what has been termed 'torture porn' – a subgenre that raises questions about the ethical limits of on-screen violence. The ethical conversation here centers on whether such explicit content desensitizes audiences or trivializes real-world violence. The films' creators have defended their work as a form of catharsis and as commentary on the value of life, illustrating the multifaceted nature of horror storytelling and the interpretative freedom that can sometimes clash with societal norms.

Stephen King's *Rage*, a novel about a school shooting, provides an introspective look at how real-world events can affect the perception of horror fiction. Following multiple school shootings in the United States, King allowed the novel to go out of print, citing ethical concerns over potential real-world implications. This act demonstrates the profound impact that external events can have on the consumption of horror literature and raises questions about the responsibility of authors in light of societal tragedies. King's decision was both a reflection on the power of storytelling and a personal stand on the ethical dissemination of content that could potentially inspire imitation.

The case of *A Serbian Film* is perhaps one of the most extreme examples of controversy in horror cinema. The film, which includes scenes of sexual violence and child abuse, has been banned or censored in various countries. The creators defended the film as a political allegory, while critics denounced it as gratuitously exploitative. Legal battles have revolved around obscenity charges and the film's availability. The discourse surrounding *A Serbian Film* showcases the tension between an artist's right to express a vision, no matter how disturbing, and the responsibility to abide by legal and ethical standards of content distribution.

In literature, Bret Easton Ellis's *American Psycho* had its share of controversy for its graphic depictions of violence, particularly against women. The novel faced calls for censorship and was published with warning labels in some countries. Legal arguments centered around free speech versus the potential for the book to incite violence. The controversy illustrates the challenging balance that the horror genre often must strike between unflinching portrayals of human depravity and the societal imperative to mitigate harm.

These cases provide valuable insights into the complex interplay of legal rights, ethical considerations, and the artistic expression intrinsic to horror fiction. They demonstrate the importance of being proactive in understanding copyright laws, the sensitivity required when engaging with disturbing subject matter, and the repercussions that the portrayal of such content can have on both creators and audiences.

As we transition to the next section, it becomes clear that writers must exercise thoughtful deliberation in their work. The legal and ethical challenges faced by creators in the horror genre underscore the need for a conscientious approach to storytelling that considers the impact of horror narratives on both individual psyches and the broader cultural milieu.

Guidance for Writers

Navigating the murky waters of legal and ethical considerations is an integral part of the horror writer's journey. Creators within this genre can look to the following guidelines as a north star to steer their creative ventures responsibly, ensuring their work is both impactful and conscientious.

Understanding Copyright Laws:
- Perform thorough research on the copyright laws relevant to your country and the jurisdictions where your work may be published or distributed.

- Create original content while being mindful of derivative works and the fine line between inspiration and infringement.

- Document your creation process meticulously to establish ownership and originality of content.

- Consult with a legal expert specialized in intellectual property to review contracts and agreements, particularly when collaborative work is involved.

- Stay updated on changes in copyright laws and legal precedents that may affect your rights as a creator.

Handling Sensitive Content with Care:
- Reflect on the purpose of your horror elements and whether they serve the story or merely exist for shock value.

- Consider the implications of depicting violence and whether it is portrayed responsibly and essential to the narrative.

- Be mindful of the societal impact your work may have, especially in relation to current events or real-life tragedies.

- Engage sensitivity readers or subject matter experts to provide feedback on your portrayal of sensitive issues.

Acknowledging Your Audience:
- Be clear about your target audience and tailor your content to be suitable for their age and sensitivity levels.

- Use content warnings judiciously to inform readers of potentially triggering material without spoiling key elements of your story.

- Foster a respectful relationship with your audience by considering their feedback and engaging in constructive dialogues about your work's impact.

Balancing Creativity and Responsibility:
- Prioritize narrative integrity while being conscientious of not perpetuating harmful stereotypes or unnecessarily graphic content.

- Encourage critical thinking and introspection rather than sensationalism or exploitation.

- Stay true to your artistic vision but remain open to making adjustments if they align better with ethical storytelling practices.

Engaging with Publishing Standards:
- Understand the editorial guidelines of publishers and platforms where your work will appear, ensuring compliance with their content policies.

- Prepare for potential self-censorship by considering alternative approaches to presenting contentious themes.

- Collaborate with editors and legal advisors to address any red flags that may arise during the publication process.

Considerations for Distribution:

- Familiarize yourself with distribution channels and their content restrictions, especially for digital media.

- Respect age ratings and content labeling systems, providing accurate information to platforms and consumers.

- Monitor your work's distribution to avoid unauthorized sharing or piracy that could undermine your legal rights and the perceived value of horror fiction.

As a horror writer, it's essential to continuously evaluate your work against these guidelines. By doing so, you ensure that you're not only protecting yourself legally but also holding yourself to a higher ethical standard. This balance is what makes horror fiction a powerful and respected form of storytelling, capable of exploring the darkest facets of human nature while illuminating the consequences and complexities inherent in our choices.

By upholding these practices, writers can contribute to the horror genre's tradition of challenging norms and evoking deep emotional responses, all while navigating the legal and ethical dimensions that accompany such formidable storytelling. This approach helps maintain horror's place as a boundary-pushing yet responsible and reflective medium in the wider landscape of fiction.

Conclusion and Future Directions

As we peer into the horizon of horror fiction's future, the terrain is both enthralling and enigmatic, rife with possibilities and perils that aspiring and established writers alike must navigate with discernment and foresight. Emerging technologies, evolving societal attitudes, and shifting legal landscapes will inexorably sculpt the genre, demanding a recalibration of how creators conceptualize and communicate their nightmares.

The Digital Realm's Influence on Creation and Consumption

The march of technology is relentless, with virtual and augmented reality poised to redefine the parameters of the horror experience. The sensory immersion these platforms afford presents an unprecedented medium for storytelling, where the lines between the fictional and the real blur perilously. This raises ethical questions: At what point does a simulated experience become too visceral, transgressing the boundary of entertainment and traipsing into psychological trauma? The potential for horror to leave lasting impressions on the psyche becomes a tangible concern in these ultra-realistic environments.

Moreover, advances in artificial intelligence may soon facilitate the automated generation of horror content, challenging the very notion of authorship. A machine that can craft tales of terror raises a plethora of copyright issues. Who owns a story penned by an algorithm trained on a dataset of human-created fiction? As these technologies mature, the legal parameters governing intellectual property rights will have to evolve accordingly, confronting the intricacies of machine learning and creative output.

Shifting Social Attitudes and Their Reflection in Horror

The malleability of social mores presents another domain of evolution for horror fiction. As societal attitudes toward topics such as mental illness, marginalized communities, and trauma evolve, so too must the way these themes are approached within the genre. Where once certain depictions might have been acceptable or overlooked, writers will now have to tread with heightened sensitivity, cognizant of the potential harm that irresponsible portrayals can inflict.

The genre's proclivity for exploring the macabre must thus be balanced with a consciousness of ethical representation. Writers will need to engage more deeply with the complexities of the human condition, employing horror not merely as a vehicle for terror but as a means to cast light on the darkness within society and the self. This entails an ongoing dialogue with diverse audiences to ensure that depictions are not just palatable but also respectful and enriching.

Legal Developments and the Internationalization of Horror

On the legal front, the global dispersion of horror fiction through digital channels compels a consideration of international copyright laws and ethical standards. As tales of terror transcend borders, they are subject to a multiplicity of legal systems, each with its own stipulations on copyright and freedom of expression. This internationalization demands from writers a more nuanced understanding of transnational legal environments, which could vary significantly from their own.

The evolution of privacy laws also plays a crucial role in the shaping of horror fiction. As real-world fears increasingly center around data exploitation and surveillance, horror writers are presented with a new wellspring of terror to draw from. However, the ethical use of personal information—even anonymized—for the creation of narratives introduces a dimension of legal consideration that must be addressed with vigilance.

The Ascent of Interactive and Community-Driven Storytelling

Interactive storytelling, facilitated by platforms like video games and online forums, offers another frontier. Here, the audience becomes a collaborator, a co-creator of the horror experience. While this shared authorship can enrich the narrative, it also presents a challenge in ensuring that community-driven content adheres to ethical and legal standards. Creators will have to design frameworks that allow for user input while safeguarding against content that could be damaging or infringing.

The proliferation of fan fiction and its legal gray areas will also be an aspect for future scrutiny. As fans take it upon themselves to expand upon established horror universes, the potential for intellectual property conflicts arises. The question becomes one of balance: How can creators maintain their rights while fostering a vibrant, engaged community that contributes to the genre's richness?

Sustainability of Horror's Cultural Significance

Finally, as horror fiction continues to captivate audiences with its exploration of fear, writers must consider the sustainability of the genre's cultural significance. This involves not only devising stories that resonate with contemporary anxieties but also ensuring that the genre evolves alongside them. By embracing inclusivity and diversity, both in narrative and authorship, horror can remain a pertinent reflection of the zeitgeist.

In the labyrinth of the future, each twist and turn presents an opportunity for horror to either reinforce its relevance or become ensnared in the webs of ethical quandaries and legal pitfalls. The choices made by writers today will echo into tomorrow, as they carve paths through the terra incognita that awaits. Whether the genre will continue to terrify and fascinate in equal measure hinges on its capacity to adapt, to be malleable without losing its essence. To maintain its edge, horror must confront the unknown with the same fervor that it asks of its readers, anticipating shifts in technology, law, and society, and embracing them as both muses and mentors in the perpetual dance with the dark.

Chapter 6

Navigating the Psychological Impact of Writing Horror

Writing horror is an intricate dance with the shadows, a journey that delves deep into the recesses of human fear, anxiety, and the darker aspects of the psyche. For horror writers, this exploration is not just an artistic endeavor but a psychological voyage that can profoundly impact their mental landscape. This chapter seeks to illuminate the nuanced relationship between crafting tales of terror and the writer's mental well-being, offering insights and strategies for navigating these shadowed waters.

The Double-Edged Sword of Imagination

Horror writers wield their imagination as both their most potent tool and their greatest adversary. The very ability that allows them to conjure chilling narratives can also blur the lines between fiction and reality, casting long shadows over their psyche.

- Emotional Resonance: The most effective horror stories are those that resonate emotionally with readers, which often means they resonate deeply with their creators first. Writers may find themselves affected by the very fears they evoke in their narratives, leading to heightened anxiety or distress.

- Vicarious Trauma: Crafting detailed scenes of terror, especially those rooted in real human fears and traumas, can lead to vicarious trauma, where writers experience emotional responses similar to those of first-hand trauma survivors.

Maintaining the Veil Between Worlds

One of the critical challenges for horror writers is maintaining a healthy separation between the dark worlds they create and their reality, ensuring that the horror on the page doesn't seep into their lives.

- Compartmentalization: Developing the ability to compartmentalize can be invaluable, allowing writers to immerse themselves in their horror narratives during the creative process and then step back into the light of the everyday world.

- Mindfulness and Grounding: Practices such as mindfulness, meditation, and grounding exercises can help writers center themselves and disengage from the intense emotions and dark themes of their work.

The Catharsis of Horror Writing

While the act of writing horror can undoubtedly have its psychological pitfalls, it also offers a unique form of catharsis, both for the writer and the reader.

- Confronting Fears: Writing horror allows authors to confront their fears in a controlled environment, turning the intangible and terrifying into something tangible that can be managed and even vanquished on the page.

- Exploration of the Human Condition: Horror writing can be a profound exploration of the human condition, delving into themes of survival, resilience, and the triumph of the human spirit in the face of darkness.

Strategies for Safeguarding Mental Health

For those who wander the shadowed paths of horror writing, safeguarding mental health is paramount. Here are some strategies to help maintain psychological balance:

- Self-Awareness: Be vigilant about monitoring your emotional and mental state, recognizing when the material you're working with is affecting you adversely.

- Create a Support Network: Build a network of fellow writers, friends, and family who understand the nature of your work and can provide support and perspective when needed.

- Professional Support: Don't hesitate to seek professional help if you find the psychological impact of your writing is becoming too challenging to manage alone. Therapists, especially those familiar with creative professions, can offer valuable strategies for coping.

- Balanced Lifestyle: Ensure that your life outside of writing includes activities and relationships that are nurturing and grounding. Physical exercise, hobbies, and time spent in nature can counterbalance the intensity of writing horror.

Writing horror is a unique artistic pursuit that requires not only creativity and skill but also a deep and often challenging engagement with the darker aspects of the human psyche. While this engagement can be psychologically demanding, it also offers a pathway to profound insights into fear, resilience, and the complexity of the human condition. By understanding the impact of writing horror on their psyche and adopting strategies to manage this impact, writers can navigate the delicate balance between exploring the darkness and maintaining their mental well-being. In the realm of horror, the pen is indeed mightier than the sword, capable of battling the monsters on the page and within, illuminating the path through the darkness with the light of human understanding and empathy.

> *"One cannot survive on coffee and coffee alone. Eat your vegetables, drink water, and make sure you get some sun (and if you're like me, a prescription for some intense vitamin D supplements)."* —**Stephanie M. Wytovich**

THE END?

Not if you want to dive into more of Crystal Lake Publishing's Tales from the Darkest Depths!

Check out our amazing website and online store or download our latest catalog here.

https://geni.us/CLPCatalog

We always have great new projects and content on the website to dive into, as well as a newsletter, behind the scenes options, social media platforms, our own dark fiction shared-world series and our very own webstore. Our webstore even has categories specifically for KU books, non-fiction, anthologies, and of course more novels and novellas.

About the Author

Joe Mynhardt stands as a paragon in the horror literary world, a Bram Stoker Award-winning South African publisher, editor, and mentor with over a decade of experience. As the founder and CEO of Crystal Lake Entertainment, Joe has transformed a humble 2012 startup into a multifaceted Intellectual Property powerhouse. Under his visionary leadership, Crystal Lake Publishing has become just one of the many thriving divisions of his company.

With a track record of working with and publishing works by luminaries such as Neil Gaiman, Clive Barker, Stephen King, Charlaine Harris, Ramsey Campbell, John Connolly, Jack Ketchum, Jonathan Maberry, Christopher Golden, Graham Masterton, Damien Angelica Walters, Adam Nevill, Lisa Morton, Elizabeth Massie, Joe R. Lansdale, Edward Lee, Paul Tremblay, and Wes Craven, Joe is the quintessential mentor for aspiring horror authors. His deep industry insights and extensive network place him in a unique position to guide both new and seasoned writers in the genre.

Joe's commitment to nurturing talent and fostering author careers is at the heart of Crystal Lake Entertainment's ethos. His approach is not just about publishing books; it's about building a community, sharing knowledge, and being a beacon of friendship and guidance in the often-intimidating world of horror writing.

Since leaving his day job in 2016 to focus full-time on his passion, Joe has also excelled as a work-from-home dad, a role he embraced in 2018. His daughter, Cayleigh, named after his childhood influences Bruce Lee and Stan Lee, is a testament to his belief in the power of storytelling across all mediums. Joe's love for great narratives extends beyond literature, encompassing comics, games, film, and television, with favorites ranging from Poe, Doyle, and Lovecraft to King, Connolly, and Gaiman.

Joe Mynhardt isn't just a figure in the horror industry—he's a driving force behind it, leading a successful online business that goes beyond the traditional boundaries of publishing. Discover more about Joe's journey and Crystal Lake's offerings at www.crystallakepub.com or connect with him on Facebook or Patreon (includes author tiers and a 7-day free trial), where he continues to inspire and lead the next generation of horror storytellers.

Readers...

Thank you for reading *Shadows & Ink Vol.2*. We hope you enjoyed this on writing guide.

If you have a moment, please review *Shadows & Ink Vol.2* at the store where you bought it.

Help other readers by telling them why you enjoyed this book. No need to write an in-depth discussion. Even a single sentence will be greatly appreciated. Reviews go a long way to helping a book sell, and is great for an author's career. It'll also help us to continue publishing quality books.

Thank you again for taking the time to journey with Crystal Lake Publishing.

You will find links to all our social media platforms on our Linktree page.
https://linktr.ee/CrystalLakePublishing

Follow us on Amazon:

MISSION STATEMENT

Since its founding in August 2012, Crystal Lake Publishing has quickly become one of the world's leading publishers of Dark Fiction and Horror books. In 2023, Crystal Lake Publishing formed a part of Crystal Lake Entertainment, joining several other divisions, including Torrid Waters, Crystal Lake Comics, Crystal Lake Kids, and many more.

While we strive to present only the highest quality fiction and entertainment, we also endeavour to support authors along their writing journey. We offer our time and experience in non-fiction projects, as well as author mentoring and services, at competitive prices.

With several Bram Stoker Award wins and many other wins and nominations (including the HWA's Specialty Press Award), Crystal Lake Publishing puts integrity, honor, and respect at the forefront of our publishing operations.

We strive for each book and outreach program we spearhead to not only entertain and touch or comment on issues that affect our readers, but also to strengthen and support the Dark Fiction field and its authors.

Not only do we find and publish authors we believe are destined for greatness, but we strive to work with men and women who endeavour to be decent human beings who care more for others than themselves, while still being hard working, driven, and passionate artists and storytellers.

Crystal Lake Publishing is and will always be a beacon of what passion and dedication, combined with overwhelming teamwork and respect, can accomplish. We endeavour to know each and every one of our readers, while building personal relationships with our authors, reviewers, bloggers, podcasters, bookstores, and libraries.

We will be as trustworthy, forthright, and transparent as any business can be, while also keeping most of the headaches away from our authors, since it's our job to solve the problems so they can stay in a creative mind. Which of course also means paying our authors.

We do not just publish books, we present to you worlds within your world, doors within your mind, from talented authors who sacrifice so much for a moment of your time.

There are some amazing small presses out there, and through collaboration and open forums we will continue to support other presses in the goal of helping authors and showing the world what quality small presses are capable of accomplishing. No one wins when a small press goes down, so we will always be there to support hardworking, legitimate presses and their authors. We don't see Crystal Lake as the best press out there, but we will always strive to be the best, strive to be the most interactive and grateful, and even blessed press around. No matter what happens over time, we will also take our mission very seriously while appreciating where we are and enjoying the journey.

What do we offer our authors that they can't do for themselves through self-publishing?

We are big supporters of self-publishing (especially hybrid publishing), if done with care, patience, and planning. However, not every author has the time or inclination to do market research, advertise, and set up book launch strategies. Although a lot of authors are successful in doing it all, strong small presses will always be there for the authors who just want to do what they do best: write.

What we offer is experience, industry knowledge, contacts and trust built up over years. And due to our strong brand and trusting fanbase, every Crystal Lake Publishing book comes with weight of respect. In time our fans begin to trust our judgment and will try a new author purely based on our support of said author.

With each launch we strive to fine-tune our approach, learn from our mistakes, and increase our reach. We continue to assure our authors that we're here for them and that we'll carry the weight of the launch and dealing with third parties while they focus on their strengths—be it writing, interviews, blogs, signings, etc.

We also offer several mentoring packages to authors that include knowledge and skills they can use in both traditional and self-publishing endeavours.

We look forward to launching many new careers.

This is what we believe in. What we stand for. This will be our legacy.

Welcome to Crystal Lake Publishing—Tales from the Darkest Depths.

www.ingramcontent.com/pod-product-compliance
Lightning Source LLC
Chambersburg PA
CBHW070057030426
42335CB00016B/1923